"Surely, all of us have experienced shattered dreams and broken relationships and the pain that can sometimes last a lifetime. In their new book, Jerry and Mary White share stories of disappointment and heartache from unfinished things: dreams, relationships, marriages. But should we continue to live in sorrow, or, as the authors suggest, can God actually direct us toward recovery and growth? I highly recommend this book, for as long as we remain on this earth, we will continue the struggle to find joy through pain."

—DR. WESS STAFFORD, president and CEO, Compassion International; author of *Too Small to Ignore* and *Just a Minute*

"All of us have something unfinished, but what to do about it and how? Jerry and Mary have taken years of incredible experiences and brought them to life in such a marvelous way that makes this book a practical guide for everyday life."

—DAVID M. BEASLEY, governor of South Carolina, 1995–1999

"Simple, not simplistic! Profound yet practical! Wise, not 'teachy'! This is a deeply good book written by two people who have been tested and refined. Whether dreams shatter or come true, God is doing His work. *Unfinished* brings hope into our uncertain lives. Thanks, Jerry and Mary."

—LARRY CRABB, PhD, Dr. Larry Crabb, best-selling author of *Inside Out*

"For each of us, there comes a day when we encounter the reality of our own earthly mortality. The finish line is in sight and the hard questions beg to be answered. In *Unfinished*, Jerry and Mary White open our eyes to where we've been, what we've done, and what is still possible in the life we have left to live. This book aligns God's plan and purpose and will deposit peace and confidence in your soul."

—TAMI HEIM, president and CEO, Christian Leadership Alliance; coauthor of *@stickyJesus: How to Live Out Your Faith Online*

"In the midst of life's competing noises, Jerry and Mary White provide straightforward and sound guidance to help us finish well. Jerry and Mary provide practical tools for allowing God's transformational power to have its way in our lives regardless of our yesterdays. What an encouragement!"

—NORMA SMITH, Washington state representative, 10th District

"Once again, Jerry and Mary White have addressed current, present issues from a personal and biblical point of view that is both inspirational and challenging. Their holistic treatment of life, wrapped in hope, will encourage and bless all who read *Unfinished*. May our belief in and reliance upon our hope in God's plan for our lives and the nations be renewed and invigorated by these timely words."

—HENRY DEENEN, president, Greater Europe Mission

"Many of us experience confusion, weariness, and wounding over the unfinished elements in our lives. In this book, Jerry and Mary White serve as guides to point the way forward. Well acquainted with grief, this couple offers help for those who suffer."

—ELISA MORGAN, author of *She Did What She Could*; publisher, FullFill.org

"Jerry and Mary White have created a very powerful tool to help us 'finish well.' Filled with practical insights, biblical illustrations, and gut-honest reflections from their own lives, this book provides a clear road map for navigating the doubts, dips, downward spirals, and disasters that most of us will inevitably face."

—ELLIE LOFARO, MA, Bible teacher;
founder, Heart Mind & Soul Ministries; author of *Leap of Faith*

"The good news is that we're not finished yet. Jerry and Mary White point the way to finishing well."

—LEITH ANDERSON, pastor emeritus,
Wooddale Church, Eden Prairie, Minnesota;
president, National Association of Evangelicals

"Jerry and Mary White address the unromantic reality of all our lives: We are unfinished. With perceptiveness and wisdom, the Whites help us move from the disappointment, discouragement, regret, confusion, and guilt that often accompany life's tough circumstances (and our own shortcomings) to give us hope and fresh perspective."

—JEAN FLEMING, author of *Feeding Your Soul* and *A Mother's Heart*

"In *Unfinished*, you will encounter eternal truths and rich wisdom that come from Jerry and Mary's real-life experiences concerning the horrible heartbreaks and dreadful disappointments life can bring to each of us. This book will give you discernment for your current situation and wise counsel for your future. The Whites will teach you how and why God so often chooses to build fruitful and effective lives on broken and busted foundations."

—WALT LARIMORE, MD,
best-selling author of *10 Essentials of Happy, Healthy People* and *Workplace Grace*

JERRY & MARY WHITE

UNFINISHED

How to Approach Life's Detours, Do-Overs, and Disappointments

Discipleship Inside Out®

NAVPRESS
Discipleship Inside Out®

NavPress is the publishing ministry of The Navigators, an international Christian organization and leader in personal spiritual development. NavPress is committed to helping people grow spiritually and enjoy lives of meaning and hope through personal and group resources that are biblically rooted, culturally relevant, and highly practical.

For a free catalog go to www.NavPress.com or call 1.800.366.7788 in the United States or 1.800.839.4769 in Canada.

ISBN-13: 978-1-61291-268-4

Cover design by Arvid Wallen
Interior images by Shutterstock

Some of the anecdotal illustrations in this book are true to life and are included with the permission of the persons involved. All other illustrations are composites of real situations, and any resemblance to people living or dead is coincidental.

Unless otherwise identified, all Scripture quotations in this publication are taken from the *Holy Bible, New International Version®* (NIV®). Copyright © 1973, 1978, 1984 by Biblica, used by permission of Zondervan. All rights reserved. Other versions used include: the *Amplified Bible* (AMP), © The Lockman Foundation 1954, 1958, 1962, 1964, 1965, 1987; *The Living Bible* (TLB), copyright © 1971, used by permission of Tyndale House Publishers, Inc., Wheaton, IL 60189, all rights reserved; THE MESSAGE (MSG). Copyright © 1993, 1994, 1995, 1996, 2000, 2001, 2002. Used by permission of NavPress Publishing Group; the New American Standard Bible® (NASB), Copyright © 1960, 1962, 1963, 1968, 1971, 1972, 1973, 1975, 1977, 1995 by The Lockman Foundation. Used by permission; *The New Testament in Modern English* (PH), J. B. Phillips Translator, © J. B. Phillips 1958, 1960, 1972, used by permission of Macmillan Publishing Company; the *Holy Bible*, New Living Translation (NLT), copyright © 1996, 2004. Used by permission of Tyndale House Publishers, Inc., Wheaton, Illinois 60189. All rights reserved; and the New King James Version (NKJV). Copyright © 1982 by Thomas Nelson, Inc. Used by permission. All rights reserved.

White, Jerry E., 1937-
    Unfinished : how to approach life's detours, do-overs, and disappointments / Jerry and Mary White.
        p. cm.
    Includes bibliographical references.
    ISBN 978-1-61291-268-4
    1. Hope--Religious aspects--Christianity. I. White, Mary, 1935- II. Title.
    BV4638.W45 2013
    248.4--dc23
                                    2012018322

Printed in the United States of America

1 2 3 4 5 6 7 8 / 18 17 16 15 14 13

*To our cherished grandchildren,
who give us great joy
as they plan and prepare
to finish their dreams and goals:*

*Zachary Thompson
Audrey Thompson
Shelby Thompson
Jordan Birch
Hannah Birch
Joshua Birch
Jerad Birch
Bryan Gray
Jamison Gray
Daniel Gray
Michael Gray*

CONTENTS

PREFACE

L ife is unpredictable, filled with twists and turns we never antici-pated. Along the way we make choices, for good or bad, that rever-berate like echoes throughout our lives. We initiate big plans and then change our minds. We dream dreams only to find them thwarted in the reality of life's circumstances. We want to do so many things. We leave so many things left undone.

The word *unfinished* paints a picture of buildings half built, of goals abandoned and incomplete, of plans interrupted by the stuff of life.

Walk with us as we explore unfinished parenting, marriage, careers, and ordinary life. Discover how to build and rebuild your dreams and how to keep going in the midst of missteps and disruptions.

But first visit Longwood Mansion with us to see an unfinished dream. Then allow us to open up the unfinished recesses of our lives. Begin to see your life in the scope of God's great plan for you.

JERRY AND MARY WHITE
Colorado Springs, Colorado

PART 1

UNFINISHED AREAS OF LIFE

CHAPTER 1

LIVING IN THE BASEMENT

Can anything be sadder than work left unfinished? Yes,
work never begun.

CHRISTINA ROSSETTI

The beautiful antebellum home, Longwood, stands on a small knoll near Natchez, Mississippi. It represents the dreams, aspirations, and plans of one man and his family.

Dr. Haller Nutt, born in 1816, couldn't imagine the unfinished plans that would haunt him throughout the final years of his life. Raised in opulent circumstances on a Mississippi plantation in the mid-nineteenth century, he had every available comfort. He received a broad education at the University of Virginia, followed by further medical studies. Throughout his life, his fertile mind explored many areas of interest and study, including agriculture, practical science, Hebrew, Greek, and medicine. Like his father before him, Haller was a physician who also loved farming. He was well known for his successful plantations, raising mostly cotton as well as all of the food necessary for his family and workers.

At age twenty-four, Haller met and married the love of his life, Julia Williams. Julia, too, came from a financially privileged family. Throughout their marriage, Haller and Julia acquired several plantations and at one point had a total of nearly eight hundred slaves. He was known as a just and caring owner who personally cared for his slaves when they were ill and who treated them kindly.

Haller was devoted to Julia and gave her extravagant gifts. One time while she was away, knowing that she loved roses, he directed his gardeners to plant ten acres of roses as a surprise for his wife. When she returned home and realized the extent of his gift, while naturally appreciative, she ruefully said that she would need the horse and buggy hitched every day to gather the roses.

Married for twenty-four years, Haller and Julia had a large family of six boys and five girls. Initially, the children were taught by governesses and tutors; Haller eventually sent them to the best schools of the day. The loss of three of their children marred the couple's happiness. A beloved daughter, Fanny, died at age two. Seven-year-old Austin was accidentally shot and killed by a cousin. Rushworth, the youngest child, was born and died in 1863. These early deaths left Haller and Julia stunned and grieving, wondering what their children would have become had they lived.

Julia had always admired the Longwood plantation in Natchez, having spent many happy times there as a child. Knowing this, Haller purchased the property when it became available and arranged for Julia to make a visit to Natchez, where he presented her with the property.

Haller and Julia chose a little knoll on which to build their dream home. Because of the mansion's unusual architecture, some neighbors called it Nutt's Folly. With the guidance of a Philadelphia architect, the Nutts designed an unusual eight-sided house, topped with a sixteen-sided cupola with an onion-shaped dome at the top. The plans included bathrooms with running water, laundry chutes, twenty-six fireplaces, twenty built-in closets, a library, a rotunda balcony around the fifth level, and an observatory on the sixth level. Haller planned for 125 windows, including floor-to-ceiling ones in the observatory. The couple purchased beautiful furnishings from around the world and had them shipped to the plantation to await completion of their mansion.

Dr. Nutt was a man with a dream. He gathered resources. He hired workers. His motivation to please his wife overrode some of the practical obstacles. Plans were conceived, drawn up, changed, revised, and put into action. The initial work began in 1858 with local builders and capable slaves. As the house progressed, expert artisans and builders arrived from Philadelphia to carry on the finer work.

When shots rang out at Fort Sumter, South Carolina, in April 1861, signaling the start of the Civil War, Haller and Julia's world was turned upside down. The Philadelphia workmen dropped their tools, bringing to a halt all of Haller's grand plans and ideas for expansion. They left all the materials and returned to the North, leaving the mansion unfinished. Only the daylight basement and the external walls of the six-story house were completed.

The basement was originally intended as housing for servants, but the Nutt family moved into the nine spacious rooms and settled in to wait out the duration of the war, completing what they could of the mansion. The expert roofer, who had fled to Philadelphia, braved the Union lines and returned to complete the roof, which no doubt saved the mansion from destruction during rains and storms.

Haller was a Union sympathizer, and the war devastated his ideals of a unified country. When the slaves were emancipated, his plantations fell into ruin and he no longer had a means of supporting himself and his family. Facing financial collapse, he despaired for his children, several of whom were still very young. In 1864, he contracted pneumonia and died a broken man, deprived of his wealth and future and living with unfinished dreams in an unfinished home. Julia always maintained that his sorrow for his country, his inability to care for his family, and his broken dreams caused his death more than the diagnosed pneumonia.

Julia was left with many young children and the challenge of feeding and caring for them in a war-torn land. The Union soldiers swept across the plantations several times, taking food, cattle, horses, and much of the building material collected for Longwood. Like many other people in the South, Julia and her children faced near starvation before the end of the war. She lived on at Longwood after the war, trying to put the family's life back together. She preserved many of her husband's medical writings and scientific information.

For many years, with the help of her son Sergeant Prentiss Nutt, Julia tried to seek justice and remuneration from the government for the destruction caused to her properties during the war. Eventually, she received a small amount—not nearly enough money to continue the work on Longwood. She lived on in the basement with an unmarried daughter and died in 1897. Her descendants continued living in the mansion basement until, finally, only a bachelor grandson lived alone in the echoing house.

"Unfinished" describes so much of the lives and dreams of Haller and Julia Nutt and their mansion, Longwood.

DREAMS VERSUS REALITY

When we visited Longwood and stood looking out from the veranda, the unfinished mansion evoked a flood of images and emotions for us: sadness, regret, memories, desires, and thoughts of what might have been, what should have been, and what may still be. We were not just thinking of the Nutts and their mansion but also of our own lives and the lives of so many of our friends. There is so much in life that we wish we could redo, so much that we can no longer do, and so much that is yet to do.

"Once upon time there lived . . ." begins the fairy tale. In childhood, we fantasize being at the center of the story—a story full of drama, danger, love, and adventure. Similarly, when we are young, we have a mental to-do list. We make great plans, have good intentions, and start to build our lives. We set out with dreams, hopes, and visions of what we might do and become. But here is where the parallel ends. In fairy tales, the story always concludes, "And they lived happily ever after." But real life is not like that. Dreams and fantasies blur and fade as reality sets in.

Some of our dreams get postponed.

Mary had to delay for many years her dream of finishing her college degree. The two of us were married after our junior year at the University of Washington, and Mary quit school to work during Jerry's final year. The plan was for her to go back to college when he graduated and entered the Air Force, but frequent moves and a growing family put that dream on hold. Finally, after twelve years and the birth of four children, Mary was able to finish her degree. A dream delayed was finally realized.

But some dreams and hopes are never realized.

Some dreams are unfinished because our plans have changed. For instance, the childhood vision of becoming a model, musician, astronaut, or firefighter fades with maturity.

Some dreams we can never finish, for we cannot turn back the clock.

Others were snatched out of our hands by people, events, divorce, the economy, war, crime, or bad choices.

We try to live with reality as it changes our dreams, yet underneath we continue to harbor aspirations to be *something*, to become *significant*. These aspirations smolder inside us, often unspoken, lingering for years. Many of us live in the basement, with our lives' superstructures unfinished. Life seems to pass us by, leaving us to wonder, wish, and survive.

Is it bad to have unfinished parts of our lives? Not necessarily.

Yet there are some things in our lives that we *must* finish. We cannot afford to leave them unfinished. We wrote this book to help you understand the difference so that with God's help, you can walk by faith, finishing what you can and accepting the things you can't.

The life of every man is a diary in which he means to write one story, and writes another; and his humblest hour is when he compares the volume as it is with what he vowed to make it. — James M. Barrie

---

The process of accomplishing achievable goals must be embedded in the reality of life and experience. Our minds may tell us one thing and our emotions another. The mixture of elation, regret, and disappointment colors our thinking. We want to settle the nagging doubt and the recurring regret. We long to set a path to the future that makes sense and is clearly led by God.

We wish the process were rational and simple, but we are complex people. Our past and present intermix in indefinable ways. In one sense, we have to "feel" our way along. In spiritual terms, we "walk by faith." Proverbs 16:9 tells us, "The mind of man plans his way, but the LORD directs his steps" (NASB). In other words, plan carefully. Work diligently. Let God put up guideposts, detour signs, and roadblocks, and follow His direction.

GET OUT OF THE BASEMENT

In the upcoming pages, we want to ponder the concept of "unfinished" and how it applies to our dreams, marriages, parenting, spirituality—and more.

We want to be practical but not simplistic. We want to be driven by hope but not be falsely enthusiastic. We want to be biblical, but we do not want to twist Scripture in any way.

We have divided the book into two parts. Part 1 addresses specific areas of life that can feel unfinished, such as marriage, career, parenting, and spirituality, and offers help for understanding what we can and cannot finish in these. Part 2 offers help for how we can finish well in all areas of our lives.

We pray that these thoughts and reflections resonate with your life and experience, as they have with ours. We've included some questions at the end of each chapter to help you bring your personal life experience to bear on the many issues. Our goals are simply:

- To view life truthfully through the lenses of Scripture and experience
- To provide insight and encouragement regarding the parts of life that are unfinished
- To help you:

  - Hope in God's master plan for your life
  - Live without regret
  - Bear brokenness and suffering
  - Put the past in perspective
  - Know when to move on

Don't keep living in the basement of your life. Take the tools offered in these pages and begin building again the life God planned for you. At the end of your life, may you be able to say along with Paul, "This is the only race worth running. I've run hard right to the finish, believed all the way."[1]

QUESTIONS FOR REFLECTION

1. What were some of your early dreams and plans?
2. What happened to them?
3. Share some of your unfinished stories.
4. What "basement" are you still living in?

CHAPTER 2

UNFINISHED DREAMS AND GOALS

Twenty years from now you will be more disappointed by the things that you didn't do than by the ones you did do. So throw off the bowlines. Sail away from the safe harbor. Catch the trade winds in your sails. Explore. Dream. Discover.

MARK TWAIN

You see things and you say, "Why?" But I dream things that never were, and I say, "Why not?"

GEORGE BERNARD SHAW

We all have dreams and hopes. As children, we dream of changing the world as a great scientist or rising to the top of the music world. During our teens, our dreams become a bit more down to earth as fantasy gives way to practical reality. As adults, our dreams begin to fade or morph into a future tarnished with excesses or shining with successes.

Our dreams stay with us; they never go away. But as reality and experience pound on us, we can be tempted to give up on them. We smile at the fantasies of children or young people, remembering all too well our own. We don't want to deny them their dreams, but we find it hard to take them seriously. Why? Could it be because we do not take our own dreams seriously?

Of course, sometimes dreams remain unfinished because circumstances superseded our earlier aspirations with even better dreams.

What were some of your early dreams? Take a moment now to write down some of your dreams. Which of them came to pass? Which remain unfinished? Which could still happen?

I had a dream my life would be so different from this hell I'm living. —lyrics from "I Dreamed a Dream"

THE IMPACT OF DREAMS

Every Christmas brings replays of the movie *It's a Wonderful Life*, in which Jimmy Stewart plays the part of George Bailey. Beaten down by the events of life, George finally gives up all his dreams. He thinks his life is of no value. As he walks to a bridge to commit suicide, he is confronted in a dream by his guardian angel, Clarence (Henry Travers). Clarence shows George what life would have been like without him. His dreams, in one sense, never came true. But his life impacted others in ways he never could have imagined.

Charles Dickens' *A Christmas Carol* also uses a dream to convey an important message to Ebenezer Scrooge. The dream reveals the blessedness of his only employee's simple life and the condemnation of his own money-grabbing existence. The dream convicts Scrooge of his selfishness and heartlessness and causes him to change and ask for forgiveness.

While these are stories, they bear resemblance to reality. Not every dream comes true. Not every dream that does not come true is a failure. Most of us do not fit the images of Scrooge or George Bailey, but their stories remind us of God's intervention in changing the directions of our goals and dreams.

WHERE DO DREAMS COME FROM?

We ask about dreams, *Is it God speaking to me, or is it just my psychological self playing tricks on me?* Most of us have had dreams that are so realistic we are sure they happened. For example:

- Jerry had a dream in which he was speaking with our son, who had been murdered years earlier. It was so real. Jerry woke up refreshed. Was it Steve? Maybe. Mary, too, had a dream about Steve. She deeply regretted not being able to say good-bye, to give him one last embrace, before his death. A few months after he died, she dreamed that he was dressed in casual clothes, walking toward her, smiling. As he approached, he gradually faded away. That dream brought her comfort and peace.
- A family member almost died in the emergency room. When he was revived, he described a beautiful, peaceful, pastoral scene with incredible music in the background. Suddenly his father, who had been gone for twenty years, appeared and asked, "Are you coming now?" The family member replied, "No, Dad. I'll be there in eleven years." A dream? A visit to heaven? Whatever the truth, this family member no longer feared death. He was unable to fully describe the peace he felt during the experience.
- When Jerry studied engineering and mathematics, he often had problems he could not solve. One night he dreamed of the solution to a difficult problem, woke up, wrote it down, and solved the problem.
- When she was a child, Mary dreamed of someday leaving her parents' farm and traveling someplace, anyplace. She wasn't unsatisfied or unhappy; she simply wanted a future that was different from her present. Where did this desire come from? Hope? Reading? A visit to the big city of Minneapolis? Years

later, when returning from one of many ministry trips overseas, she remarked, "I used to pray for trips like this. I think I forgot to turn off the request!"

So, again, where do our dreams come from?

God is the ultimate source of our dreams and goals. He uses our minds, awake or asleep, to implant ideas. Ephesians 3:20 speaks of His acting through and beyond our human dreams and goals, through things that we "imagine": "to him who is able to do immeasurably more than all we ask or imagine, according to his power that is at work within us." Other versions use the word *think*. The Living Bible uses *dream of*. The Greek word *noeo* means "consider, perceive or think."

God implants ideas in unusual ways. In the Bible, He often used dreams and visions to communicate with people. Daniel had visions of things to come. John, in the book of Revelation, saw the end of an age and the ultimate victory of God and Christ. The apostle Paul was converted through a dream and later led by another dream.

God sometimes uses people — relatives, teachers, friends, mentors — to impact and influence us and sow dreams in our hearts. They help us believe in our dreams; they believe in *us*.

Jerry's only exposure to someone who had gone to college was an uncle, whom he grilled mercilessly to find out what college was like. Jerry had somehow imagined himself going to college. Where did the desire come from? None of Jerry's friends even talked about it. Did he have any sense of destiny? No. At the time, he was emerging as a fairly good high school student. Because he was good in math, he tried to read a short book on Einstein's theory of relativity. He didn't get beyond the first few pages before the mathematics went far beyond his learning, but he still wanted to understand. He suddenly realized he could do something more with his life.

Two people encouraged him to fulfill this dream of going to college. Bob Shepler, the businessman who introduced him to Jesus, attended only one year of college, yet he encouraged Jerry to go. When Jerry entered the University of Washington, Bob drove him three hundred miles across the state to enter the university, and he helped Jerry financially in his first year of study.

The second encourager was a high school history teacher, Mr. Louis Livingston. He gave Jerry a C in his class when Jerry was a freshman. In his senior year, when he had another class with Mr. Livingston, Jerry determined to do well. One day after he gave a report on the battle of Appomattox in the Civil War, Mr. Livingston said, "Now, that's the way a report should be given." That statement has stuck with Jerry all his life. Mr. Livingston validated that Jerry could learn and succeed. Jerry kept connected to him until he died at age 107.

Other times God simply puts an idea in our minds. The idea of this book was planted as we stood on the veranda of Longwood. We were not looking for an idea; it just appeared in our minds.

Often we refer to this as God putting something on our hearts. God "spoke" to Jerry as he was interacting with a neighbor at Cape Canaveral, Florida. Jerry asked him what he planned to do for his next Air Force assignment, and he said he wanted to go to the Air Force Academy to teach. Although we had planned on leaving the Air Force, God used this conversation to put in our minds and hearts the idea of being on the faculty of the Air Force Academy, where we could reach students with the gospel and get further discipling and training from The Navigators. (The Navigators' headquarters is just a few miles from the Air Force Academy in Colorado Springs.) That dream came to pass about four years later with a number of detours, discouragements, and miracles. We held it with an open hand, asking God to allow it only if that were His direction.

Earlier we asked you to write down some of your dreams. Now write down how those dreams came into your mind.

Through the years, many people have come to us with their visions and dreams. Some dreams are wild and seemingly impossible or at least improbable. Others are as simple as changing careers, getting more education, starting a small evangelistic outreach, or writing a book. We always listen carefully for that spark that indicates that the idea comes from God and not just the person's own ambitions.

One man, a distinguished professor and department head at a large university, told us he had a dream to reach young people for Christ by using fly-fishing as his platform. He retired and is doing that right now. No one outside his town will ever know of his imaginative evangelism, but he saw the need, knew his own interest and skill, and began to dream how God could use them.

Another friend had a desire to write and minister to women. She had a baby late in life, when her other children were nearing college age. She went through a time of depression and struggle with her significant life change. But it was that very experience that has led her to write, publish books and articles, and minister to women in many contexts.

UNFULFILLED — YET

A couple of questions emerge in our considerations of unfinished dreams and goals:

1. Why don't people fulfill their dreams? Although many reasons impact each individual case, the primary causes come from either external or internal sources.

Externally, we experience circumstances we cannot control: the economy, accidents, health, and the actions of others. Any of these can deflect, delay, or destroy our dreams and plans.

Internally, we make choices to change or rethink our directions. God may lead us to abandon older dreams for new ones. Many of us make priority choices to do one thing and not another. No law says that we must pursue every dream or goal to its conclusion. We can change. God can redirect us.

2. How should we look at our unfulfilled dreams? A friend recently asked, "Did I misread God?" He had experienced a reversal in his life about something he felt had been a leading from God and was wondering how to respond.

If, like our friend, you believe that God has given you a dream but that dream has not been fulfilled, what should you do? This is the time to walk by faith. God's plan for living or dying is stated in 2 Corinthians 5:7: "We live by faith, not by sight." We dream, think, and plan but then look to God to lead us step-by-step. "In his heart a man plans his course, but the LORD determines his steps."[1]

It's important to remember that none of us can definitely know if a dream is God's assured direction for us until we see it come to pass. But rest assured that *if* a dream comes from God, it will be fulfilled — eventually. Sometimes we have to wait a long time before we see a dream fulfilled.

This was certainly the case for Joseph, the eleventh son of Jacob. As a young boy, Joseph had two dreams. In one dream, sheaves of grain bowed to his sheaf. In the other, the sun, moon, and stars bowed down to him. He had no clue what the dreams meant, so he told his father and brothers. They understood them immediately. They said to him, "You foolish boy. What arrogance makes you say that we will all bow down to you?" And they hated him.[2]

Later, his brothers captured him in the desert, planning to kill him. Instead, they sold him as a slave to Midianite traders, who later sold him to Potiphar, a leader in Pharaoh's government in Egypt. After Joseph succeeded as a slave, Potiphar's wife falsely accused him of molesting her when he refused her sexual invitations. Thrown into prison, he met two servants of Pharaoh's who had dreams. He, with God's help, interpreted them correctly. The baker was hanged and the cupbearer (wine and food taster, protector of the pharaoh) was exonerated.

Later Pharaoh had two dreams. No one could interpret them. The cupbearer remembered Joseph and told Pharaoh about him. "Get him," commanded Pharaoh. Joseph interpreted the dreams as seven years of incredible harvests followed by seven years of famine. After hearing the wisdom of Joseph, Pharaoh made him prime minister. Joseph still did not know what his earlier dreams meant. Nine years later and twenty-three years from his original dreams, his brothers came seeking food and bowed down to him. Then he understood.[3]

Real dreams, a real word from God, yet twenty-three years came and went before they were fulfilled. Joseph did not know the full meaning of his dreams until he saw his brothers in Egypt asking for grain.

Just because a dream is unfilled now doesn't mean it won't be fulfilled in the future. We can be confident that God will lead us as we pursue our dreams and goals. This truth can keep us going and motivated. Even with detours and disappointments, we can be certain of God's ultimate care and direction.

QUESTIONS FOR REFLECTION

1. Share a dream or goal you once had that now seems impossible.
2. What events, decisions, or circumstances have delayed or erased the possibility of achieving your dream or goal?
3. Were your dreams unrealistic? Where did they come from? Were they founded in God or were they just a part of your imagination and desires? Does it matter?
4. What can you do now to bring new dreams alive?

CHAPTER 3

UNFINISHED MARRIAGES

A happy marriage is like a long conversation that seems too short.

ANDRÉ MAUROIS

Do you remember some of the dreams and plans from when you were first married? You and your spouse talked, discussed, and worked toward a significant and shared future. Your plans were driven by love and passion. Your dreams were something you lived for and worked toward together.

How has your marriage lived up to those dreams? Which dreams for your marriage were fulfilled? Which dreams got replaced, rightly so? Which dreams and hopes for your marriage remain unfinished?

Over the years, we have observed three types of unfinished marriages: (1) those that drag along for years with indifference or hostility on the part of one or both spouses, (2) those that end in divorce, and (3) those that end with the death of a beloved spouse. All of these conditions bring sadness and misery to the couple, their children, and their extended family and friends. Even though divorce and death bring finality to a marriage, the marriage remains unfinished in that the couple's dreams and plans are never realized. Those hopes remain unfinished, although the remaining partner can eventually arrive at a place of acceptance and peace.

Let's take a closer look at each of these and see what insight Scripture can bring to couples in one of these predicaments.

UNFINISHED BY DISSENSION

Some marriages are so bad that the husband and wife barely tolerate each other. Quarreling, tension, and silence dominate the home.

Gary and Abby were one such couple. Married for more than forty years, their gradually deteriorating relationship created a tense, combative home. Their grown children avoided them because they did not want to be drawn into their parents' demands that they choose sides.

Although Gary and Abby professed a faith in God, they failed to go deep in that faith, and even in their church situation their hostility showed. Gary ignored Abby's constant nagging, except for occasional brief accusations and taunts that caused her to retaliate with more whining and harassing. The vicious circle continued, poisoning family and friends alike. Then Gary developed a liver disease and died a year later. Without her partner to harass, Abby seemed to lose interest in life and died a few months later. It was a sad end to what could have been a good relationship if only they had been able to work and pray together toward resolution.

This couple plowed ahead in their marriage in spite of the conflict, isolation, disrespect, and misery. When dissension rules a marriage, peace and harmony and happiness have no chance. And everyone around the couple is caught up in the conflict. No one who observes a feuding couple is drawn to Jesus and the demonstration a husband and wife are to give of Christ and His church.

We were reminded of this when we traveled to a conference with a couple about our age that we knew only slightly. For the entire three-hour trip, they bickered. She corrected his driving. He told her to shut up. They tried to tell us about their family, and neither could agree on details that were of no importance. He was a Republican and she was a

Democrat, and they worked that over for many miles. They never agreed on one thing that we could remember. They tried to draw us into taking sides, although if we made an innocuous statement of some kind, they moved so quickly to the next argument that it didn't matter if we responded or not. Finally, as we approached the conference grounds, she yelled at him to stop the car. In a rage, she slammed out of the car and walked the last quarter mile. Those three hours with them were the most uncomfortable we have spent in a long time.

How tragic! There is a poignant sadness in a marriage ruled by dissent. Every couple begins a marriage with high hopes for happiness, contentment, and joy. When bickering controls a relationship, those goals are never reached and the marriage feels unfinished and bitter.

Is it healthy for the spouses or the children to exist in such unhappiness? Of course not. Scripture has some things to say to couples who are always battling with each other. Applying these insights significantly reduces this kind of destructive interaction:

You should practice tenderhearted mercy and kindness to others. Don't worry about making a good impression on them but be ready to suffer quietly and patiently. Be gentle and ready to forgive; never hold grudges. Remember, the Lord forgave you, so you must forgive others. Most of all, let love guide your life.[1]

Dear brothers, don't be too eager to tell others their faults, for we all make many mistakes. . . . If anyone can control his tongue, it proves that he has perfect control over himself in every other way.[2]

When the battles begin:

- **Practice humility and patience.** Instead of arguing with your spouse, say, "You may be right." This is an ideal way to defuse arguments. It allows each member of the warring party to step back, regroup, and retain some dignity.

- **Pray together.** This is very difficult to do in a pitched battle, but it works. Be the first to suggest prayer, even silent prayer together if neither partner is able to voice a prayer.
- **Seek help** from wise friends, from your pastor, or from a professional counselor. Do not enlist family and friends who will take sides and exacerbate the dissension.

If your marriage is full of dissension, determine to change it. It is never too late. Whether you have been married for five months, five years, or fifty years, God can intervene and bring change and harmony to your relationship.

UNFINISHED BY DIVORCE

No one begins their marriage expecting it to end in divorce, yet nearly half of the marriages in the U.S. end this way. Some people experience two, three, or more failed marriages.

Every divorce has unique roots. Every divorce has deep hurts and ramifications that radiate into the lives of those involved for years to come. Often the ripple effect seems silent, but, like a tsunami, it wreaks havoc in so many lives. Families and friends feel forced to choose sides.

Marriages that end in divorce have many unfinished aspects:

- **The relationships will not be repaired or rebuilt.** Even when civility exists between the separating spouses, rebuilding is rare.
- **The couple's children will be scarred by the divorce,** regardless of the family's best efforts to shield and protect them. Shuttling between homes only highlights the unfinished nature of the family. If the children are very young when the divorce happens, they may feel responsible for the breakup.

    Jerry and his stepbrothers grew up wondering why they had different surnames. Their mother never explained this puzzle or the cause of her divorce from Jerry's father. It was a part of her past that was too painful to discuss. However, to her credit, she remained good friends with her former husband's mother. Grandma was a special lady who profoundly influenced Jerry right up to the time of her death at age ninety-three.

- **The financial security for both the man and the woman is disturbed and perhaps jeopardized.** Even in the best separations and divorce agreements, divorce can leave both parties impoverished.

There are legitimate divorces, of course. Spouses who have experienced abuse and infidelity justifiably flee for their protection and sanity. And many remarriages are healthy and fulfilling.

But even when divorce is warranted, its negative consequences can reverberate for years. We have many friends who came to faith later in life, and in their second marriages they readily acknowledge the adverse impact of divorce. If they have children from a previous marriage, they work hard to heal the unfinished consequences.

If you are contemplating divorce because you are in an unpleasant and embattled marriage, we urge you to prayerfully consider the many ways this decision will negatively impact you and many others. Although divorce may seem a simple answer to your marriage struggles, it brings unimagined negative consequences in the years ahead. The hard work of repairing and restoring a beleaguered marriage will help you avoid the sad cost of divorce.

UNFINISHED BY DEATH

Maria and Richard had been married for eight years and had three small children when he was diagnosed with liver cancer and died within five months. Maria lived with the grief of a husband lost too soon. She said, "Oh, we didn't have enough time. Not enough time." Yet her life had to go on. Her children, too, lived with grief and needed her help and support.

When Jerry's mother died at the age of sixty-two, his stepfather remarked, "We were such good friends. We got along so well." He used to sit on the couch in their little family home, saying he wished they had more time together. He and Mother had made plans to travel after his retirement from a physically demanding job. That dream remained unfinished with the onset of her cancer. The pop-up camper they had purchased stayed in storage. Trips they had dreamed of were never taken.

Widows and widowers live with many unfinished plans and dreams. Whether the death was sudden or anticipated, hopes for the future are never realized. Even when the marriage is of long duration, the parting is painful. One man, widowed after sixty-seven years of marriage, said, "We had so many things we wanted to do together." Unfinished.

The death of a spouse is inevitable. One friend says, "At some point, one of us will lay the other in the arms of Jesus." While we don't want to contemplate this parting, we need to accept and prepare for the separation. Sometimes the parting is sudden. Sometimes there is time for an extended good-bye. Either way, we need the comfort and strength of God to face the grief.

We also need practical skills so we can take up the slack caused by the absence of a trusted partner. Spouses need to discuss and understand the family finances, domestic tasks, and children's needs and even make funeral preparations.

When Mary's stepmother died, all arrangements had been made for her funeral, and all expenses were prepaid. She had planned her memorial service in detail, from what songs to sing to the number of verses. Her husband's health was failing and her thoughtful preparations relieved the family of many difficult and sad decisions. The family was able to grieve without the weight of immediate decisions.

What are some healthy ways to bear the grief of losing a precious spouse and renew some equilibrium in your life?

- **Pace yourself.** Grief is hard work. Conserve your physical and emotional energy.

- **Delay major changes in your life.** Rational thinking is at a low ebb during grief.
- **Lean into the pain.** Ignoring it or covering it with frantic activity will only delay acknowledging the severity of your loss.
- **Welcome help from those who love you.** Practical help, emotional support, and spiritual support will carry you through difficult days.
- **Refuse to live with regrets.** You may review things you would have done differently, but try to concentrate on the good memories and be thankful for what God gave you.

EVEN IN GOOD MARRIAGES . . .

Of course, there are good marriages, fantastic marriages, that last with joy for a lifetime. But no marriage is without conflict. We do not want to paint a picture so idealistic that it does not bear up under the scrutiny of reality.

Couples in good marriages also experience times of tension and conflict, but they choose to work through them, generously giving way when conflicts can't reach resolution. They do not allow their differences to sever their marriage or dim their love.

Good marriages also have aspects that are unfinished; there is always more to learn and do in the areas of communication, closeness, and teamwork.

We have been married for more than five decades, but we are still very different in some areas, including our internal clocks. Jerry reaches his peak toward evening, while Mary is alert and busy at 5:00 a.m. This difference has caused numerous areas of needed compromise over the years. At what time do we pray together? When one is half-asleep? What time of day do we compare our schedules? When one can barely put together a comprehensive thought? This may seem a simple thing, but this one difference has demanded both of us to offer the other understanding and cooperation.

Marriage is the most intimate of human relationships. If divorce and death don't intervene, it will be the longest relationship you ever have. Live, with God's help, in such a way that your days are filled with joy and contentment and your memories bring no regrets.

QUESTIONS FOR REFLECTION

1. What areas in your marriage remain unfinished?
2. What steps can you take to heal broken places in your marriage?
3. What idiosyncrasies that irritate you can you overlook in your spouse?
4. How can you strengthen spiritual communication with your spouse?
5. What does it mean to extend grace to your spouse?

CHAPTER 4

UNFINISHED PARENTING

Making the decision to have a child is momentous. It is to decide forever to have your heart go walking around outside your body.

ELIZABETH STONE

Erma Bombeck, the beloved humorist of the late twentieth century, said that when her grown children were walking down the aisle to marry, she wanted to follow along, shouting, "Wait, I'm not finished with you yet!"

We chuckle because we can relate. Every parent has one more idea to implant in their children's minds, one more bit of advice to convey, one more suggestion to make, one more area of their children's training to complete. Even the most admirable children can cause parental concern—and it doesn't stop when our children become adults. It's not uncommon to hear parents lament,

- "I wish I could help him make a decision about his future, but those days are past."
- "She never did listen to me, and now she's made a mess of her life."
- "He moved out the minute he turned eighteen, and I would give anything to hug him and hear his loud music and banging doors again."

- "I did so many things wrong when they were growing up. How can I make amends now?"

The truth is that some aspects of parenting will always remain unfinished. We never stop feeling responsible. We never quit or give up. We will always feel that we could have or should have done more. We never stop being a parent. But as true as that might be, we must live in the present. Our comfort is in knowing we are doing all we can and that we have surrendered our children to God.

STAGES OF PARENTING

There is a hierarchy of concerns for parents. We hope that our children will grow and develop and gain independence, and we trust that they will reach adulthood unscathed from the devastating effects of promiscuity, drugs, and malicious friends. One set of parents worry and grieve that their son is incarcerated for dealing drugs, while another mom and dad fret that their daughter didn't make the dean's list in college. Both sets of parents feel they are hanging in the balance, waiting to see what track their child's life will take. This uncertainty makes some parents feel out of control and desperate. What is the best way for parents to approach these concerns? It depends on the age of the child.

Years ago we developed the illustration on the following page to indicate the four stages of parenting.[1] As you can see, the kind of parenting required changes over the years. Parental control becomes less and less as a child grows and matures. (Keep in mind that individual children progress at their own rate.)

When children are little, ages zero to seven, they need their parents' complete care and love. During this period of their lives, we give our kids directives and commands, always, we hope, covered by love. We control our children in order to teach, protect, and guide them, but that control diminishes quickly as they grow.

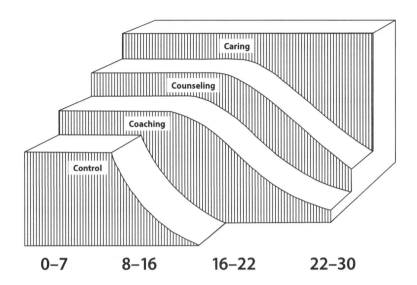

| 0-7 | 8-16 | 16-22 | 22-30 |

As they mature into puberty and adolescence, children need their parents to move to a coaching and counseling style of parenting. Many of us try to control our children much longer than we should. We often control out of fear that our children will make ruinous decisions. We worry about their choices of friends, their spending habits, the possibility of addictions, and their values and decision-making skills. Our fear is a reflection of our perceived parenting failures. Such thinking only leads to frustration for both parent and child.

Parents often experience major wake-up calls when children reach adolescence, are midway through the teens, and first reach adulthood. During these periods, parenting ground is shifting sand because children are making rapid adjustments to the next stage of their development.

As children reach the age of sixteen, our trust in them should increase. We must also work on keeping communication going. This means more listening than talking. We cannot know our children's thinking processes unless we listen to them without judging and advising. We want them to grow up to be independent, capable, wise adults. A friend has often said, "We are working ourselves out of a job."

Once our children become adults, we can only love them and pray for them. Whether the issues our adult children face are minor or major, we must let them make their own decisions and face the consequences. We can support and encourage them, but we cannot control them. We cannot force ourselves into their lives. The older they get, the less we can intervene. Unsolicited advice often meets with resistance and ridicule. If we wait to be asked for counsel, it is much more likely to be received and followed.

It's easy for parents to miss the clues and signals that it's time to move to the next stage of parenting. For that reason, it is important for you as a parent to review and prepare yourself for what you can expect during each stage. As you grow in spiritual maturity and experience, so will your parenting.

GENERATIONAL DIFFERENCES

Children are growing up faster with each generation. They are exposed to situations their parents never faced. They have more opportunity to access information, both helpful and horrific, through means that were unimaginable in the previous generation. It's almost impossible for parents to protect their children from exposure to destructive influences. All of these pressures can interrupt and destroy family harmony.

As children enter adolescence, parents need to understand the environment in which their kids are growing up and acknowledge that it is quite different from the one the parents grew up in. Whether they're three or forty-three, our kids are of a different generation than we are, with different values and perspectives. Sociologists who study the generations can give us clues to understanding these realities. There are many studies available on generational information. The chart on the next page does a good job of summarizing generational differences.

We must try to understand our children's thinking and motivations rather than expect them to understand ours. They are concentrating on

Excerpts from
GENERATIONAL DIFFERENCES
Compiled by Dennis Gaylor
Director, Chi alpha Campus Ministries, USA
April 2002[2]

	Traditionalists	Baby Boomers	Generation X	Millennials
Birth Years	1900–1945	1946–1964	1965–1980	1981–2000
Current Age	63–86	44–62	28–43	8–27
Famous People	Bob Dole, Elizabeth Taylor	Bill Clinton, Meryl Streep	Barak Obama, Jennifer Lopez	Ashton Kutcher, Serena Williams
Messages That Motivate	Your experience is respected	You are valued You are needed	Do it your way Forget the rules	You will work with other bright, creative people
Motivated By	Being respected Security	Being valued, needed Money	Freedom and removal of rules Time off	Working with other bright people Time off
Communication	Discreet	Diplomatic	Blunt/direct	Polite
View of Authority	Respectful	Impressed	Unimpressed	Relaxed
Preferred Work Environment	Conservative	"Flat" organizational hierarchy	Functional, positive, fun	Collaborative

forging their lives. Children don't care where their parents are coming from. Although cultural environments change, as Mary's mother always said, "Times change, but human nature doesn't."

PARENTAL PAIN

It's inevitable that parents will experience pain. Scripture tells us that as long as there have been families on the earth, there has been hurt. The Bible is filled with stories of unfinished families that split apart, hated each other, failed to forgive, and even killed one another.

Consider the first family. Genesis 4 records the troubled relationships that Adam and Eve experienced in their family. They welcomed sons Cain and Abel but lived to see Abel murdered by Cain, and then God banished Cain to wander for a lifetime. An unfinished family, indeed, experiencing a lifetime of sorrow and estrangement. But eventually God brought comfort and hope by giving Adam and Eve another son, Seth, and more sons and daughters. However broken a family, God's healing is possible. There is always hope for change.

King David's family also demonstrates the unfinished nature of many families. David was successful as a warrior, national leader, poet, spiritual example, and musician, but his success as a parent is questionable. The Old Testament clearly describes the disasters that plagued the lives of his children: incest, betrayal, murder, jealousy, and sibling rivalry. His children's relationships deteriorated as he grew older, and he died without seeing his children reconciled. Although David would have been proud to see the wisdom and grace with which Solomon ruled after him, his grandson Rehoboam was a vicious and oppressive ruler.

Truly, David's was an unfinished and fractured family. But even though his family displayed such problems, the Bible records David's relationship with God as intimate, trusting, and loving. God allowed David to be an ancestor of the Messiah in spite of his human failures.

Few contemporary families endure the amount of pain and trauma that these families suffered, but all parents feel some degree of regret and chagrin as they watch their children grow and develop. All parents want their children, young or mature, to avoid costly life-changing mistakes and poor decisions. But adult children live their own lives. They may choose a lifestyle and relationships that bring untold hurt to their parents. They may even choose to attack and accuse their parents and break off the relationship.

At a conference not long ago, an elderly couple approached us and asked if they could tell us their story. They had daughters with distinct personalities. One had a defiant, resistant character, and although the couple tried to express their love and concern and prayed for her consistently, she left home as quickly as she could legally do so. Over the years, their relationship slowly improved, but in her thirties, the daughter felt overwhelmed with anger and resentment. She began to see a therapist who suggested that she had been molested as a child and that the molester was her father.

Without evidence and void of compassion, the daughter accused her father and implicated her mother. Eventually, she convinced one of her sisters to join her in the allegations. The dazed parents stood before us, weeping and heartbroken. The family they envisioned for their last years had disappeared, and they had no hope of it being renewed. They live with the painful reality of an unfinished family.

When devastation like this hits parents, there is a period of shock and grief; the support and comfort of trusted friends or counselors can be healing and instructive. Hurting parents need care and confidentiality during painful family trials, so be careful to distinguish the difference between curious friends and caring friends. There may never be relational healing, but there can be acceptance, release of the child, and peace for the parents. This may take a long time but must be the goal for sorrowful parents.

As parents, we never stop praying and hoping for our children to live long, content, and contributing lives. Family disagreements may remain unresolved, but we can continue to pursue reconciliation. Time has a way of healing and soothing past differences. God's purpose is to bring peace and harmony in all relationships.

Once a parent, always a parent. Once a child, always a child. —Unknown

---

HOPE FOR A FRESH START

None of us is a perfect parent. Every parent begins parenting with no experience. There is no practice or dress rehearsal. The good news is that we can deal with regrets and the what-ifs of past parenting. Although we cannot redo the past, we can make changes and a fresh start.

Tony and Jan were well into their late thirties when they heard the good news of Jesus' love and turned their hearts to God. Their three teenage children were perplexed by the abrupt change in their parents' attitude toward life. As they reached adulthood, two of the children finally followed their parents into a new life in Christ, but one son rejected not only his parents' new spirituality but them as well. He forged a new life for himself, becoming financially successful but rarely contacting his parents or siblings. Tony and Jan occasionally read about him in the local newspaper, as he achieved another measure of success in the business world, but they were brokenhearted by their son's absence from the family. They made many overtures to reconcile with him.

At this point, he has refused to reunite with the family. Tony and Jan have pleaded with the Lord to have their son back, but the decision to accept them and their relationship with God remains with their son. Tony and Jan have not given up hope for reconciliation. They have enlisted much prayer for their son, they confide in a few trusted friends, and they regularly consult with a counselor who directs them toward positive avenues of thought and activity.

One of the best things parents can do is pray for their children and be patient. We can't force a relationship with our kids, but God's Spirit can, over time, heal and rebuild those relationships.

Several years ago, there was a story circulating on the Internet about a young man who left home embittered and resentful toward his parents whom he felt were too demanding and restrictive. He refused to communicate with them and built a life he thought he wanted. After several years, he realized how rash he had been in severing ties with his parents. He wrote an apologetic and humble letter, asking their forgiveness. He said that he would be returning to their town on a certain date and that if they would forgive him and agree to see him to please put a white handkerchief in the front window. On the appointed day, he arrived in front of his parents' home to find white handkerchiefs, tablecloths, bed sheets, and towels hanging from every window. The power of apology and forgiveness conquered the bitterness of many years.

This story closely parallels the story of the prodigal son, one of the most beautiful stories in any literature. It is detailed in Luke 15:11-32. A father with two sons offered his inheritance to them. The younger accepted, ran off, and wasted his money in dissolute living. He returned repentant and humble. His father joyously received him and prepared a party to celebrate. The older son in a jealous rage rebuked the father, and we have no record that the older son responded to his father's pleading for grace in the family situation.

Perhaps you are a young person reading this and have resentments and anger toward your parents that you cannot forget or forgive. Consider the long-term consequences of not releasing the hurts of the past. Words spoken can never be retrieved. We have no guarantees of a future, and the possibility of restoration can be severed in an instant.

MOVING FORWARD

Parenting is such a huge and complex undertaking that we can't possibly give it full treatment in one chapter. It is a lifelong process that sometimes feels finished as children progress well but all too often seems unfinished as their difficulties and mistakes drag us into an emotional, painful quagmire while we wait for them to change. As long as life endures, we have hope that parents and children and siblings will be reconciled and see their relationships as complete and strong.

So how can you move forward in your parenting in a way that minimizes the likelihood of future regret?

- Enlist trusted friends to pray for your children and for you.
- Release your children from your control and unsolicited advice.
- Pray for godly mentors who can help guide your children through adolescence and early adulthood.
- Be willing to wait for God to work in your children's lives.
- Resist interfering in their decisions.
- Pray, pray, pray and wait for the final outcome.

Remember that no two children are identical in their needs and personalities. Keep learning and trying to understand the thinking, motivation, and needs of each of your children. And remember that there is no limit to what God can do.

QUESTIONS FOR REFLECTION

1. How can you work toward restoring relationships with your children?

2. How can you enlist others to pray for the unfinished relationships in your family and yet maintain confidentiality?

3. What can you do to understand the environment and thinking of younger generations?

4. Should the younger or older generation bear the most responsibility for finishing tattered relationships? Why?

CHAPTER 5

UNFINISHED CAREERS

*Living between what should have been, what ought to
be, and what might be.*

JERRY WHITE

Work, whether in the marketplace or at home, consumes about
60 percent of our waking hours. It frames both our egos and
our survival, as it often affects our identity and our ability to provide for
ourselves and our families. It's a critical part of what gives our lives
meaning.

Most people work, but not everyone enjoys their work. For some,
work is a drudging necessity to put bread on the table. For others, work
is a career—a pursuit or occupation that defines them and gives satisfying fulfillment.

What are the differences between work, a job, and a career? A career
is defined by the primary work we do over a significant part of our lives;
for example, we may have a career as a plumber, engineer, salesperson,
or teacher. We can have more than one career. Most careers involve
many jobs. Work is what we do in our jobs and careers.

Our parents' generation averaged one career and two to three
jobs. Our generation had two careers and three to five jobs. The
succeeding generation engaged in three to four careers and five to ten
jobs. This trend places great uncertainty in our lives. Consequently,

most people never finish a career. Instead, a new one evolves or is created.

In this chapter, we want to address those whose work, jobs, or careers have been disrupted, redirected, or destroyed for a variety of reasons. We will discuss how you can view areas of work that seem unfinished and will encourage you to develop an altered plan. Most of all, we want to help you see God's broader plan. We want you to trust and not give up.

Let's look now at what causes careers and work to be unfinished.

THE INEVITABLE INTERRUPTIONS

Most of us can remember being asked as children, "What do you want to be when you grow up?" Perhaps we replied, "Oh, maybe a fireman, or an astronaut." "Maybe an actress or a dancer." But even when we think we know how we want to spend our working lives, often things don't turn out the way we initially planned.

In the course of our working lives, sidetracks and disappointments are inevitable. Some of these career transitions are planned. They are personal choices to move, change jobs, or change careers. One young couple we know decided to leave the military after nine years and three deployments. The separations were adversely affecting their family and marriage. But when he left the military, he found himself out of work in a down economy. They made the right choice, but even so, his work life was filled with uncertainty.

Other career transitions are unplanned, which makes them even more challenging. These interruptions can be caused by failure, dismissal, and self-inflicted circumstances.

Failure. Jerry entered the U.S. Air Force immediately following college graduation with the dream and goal of being a pilot. He was assigned to Spence Air Base near Moultrie, Georgia, and enjoyed the fun and success of flying the T-34 and T-28 prop training aircraft for six months. Then he went on to the final phase of pilot training in the T-33 jet at Webb Air Force Base near Big Spring, Texas. The runway was so hot you could fry eggs on it. All was going well. Jerry had never failed a check ride.

Near the end of the training, he learned to fly two-ship formation. On the day of his check ride in formation flying, Jerry pointed out that one wheel strut was low, but his instructor said it was within limits. As the jet lifted off the runway, it was caught in the jet wash of the lead plane, causing the plane to dip one wing dangerously, which scared the living daylights out of Jerry and his check pilot. They finally joined the lead, but Jerry flew badly, and when they landed he was given a pink slip. He failed the check ride.

A few days later, he flew a re-check ride and did okay, but when he landed, the instructor pilot failed him again although he had flown moderately well. Three days later, an evaluation board met and decided that Jerry was out of the program—an abrupt end to his career as a pilot.

When our careers are interrupted like this, we wonder, *Could I have studied more? Could I have focused and prepared better mentally for the check ride?* Such questions are almost unanswerable, and we are wise not to expend our energy trying to answer them.

So what did we do? Although disappointed and discouraged, we prayed that God would lead us to the future. The truth is that God had other plans for our lives. They were better plans, but we did not know it at the time. We plan and work, but God directs and detours.

Layoffs. Most people face some discouragement and disappointment in their work. The economy goes up and down, affecting the job market. When the economy is in a tailspin, it affects housing, construction, real estate, retail, and more. Corporate decides to close offices and plants, to downsize, to meet new markets, and many are caught up in the aftermath.

Economic turndowns force layoffs. As we were writing this, a fine young Air Force captain told us he was being riffed (RIF: reduction in force) because of an overage in his career field. Another young woman we know, a single mom, went for years with no suitable full-time employment although she was well qualified.

Of course, layoffs come about for many reasons. Age and experience affect our ability to find work; we may be too young, too old, over-qualified, or under-qualified. Who wants to hire a fifty-eight-year-old engineer? Where can a pilot with twenty-five years of experience go when the airline he works for declares bankruptcy? How can a woman return to the workforce after being a stay-at-home mom for twenty years?

For many, layoffs like these are devastating. Some people go into depression. Some give up. Some lose their homes. Many take minimum-wage jobs just to get by. Some move back in with their parents. Others adjust and make necessary changes.

That's what Arnie, a builder of high-end homes, did. A combination of a disastrous fire and a failing economy forced him into bankruptcy. Though devastated, he and his family adjusted by moving to a smaller home and making changes in their lifestyle. He developed remodeling businesses while at the same time investigating new opportunities. His former experiences as an engineer aided in developing his own business.

Self-inflicted circumstances. Sometimes our worst enemy is ourselves. We make mistakes, misjudgments, and decisions that affect us for a lifetime. We neglect studies in high school or college; perhaps we dabble in drugs and alcohol or choose to be lax in our job. This creates a deficit that is difficult to overcome or undo in the future. Many of these choices are made in our youth or our pre-Christian days. While we can never undo what we have done in the past, we can, with great effort, surmount our mistakes.

Roy and Daniel were two young men who were dismissed from the U.S. Air Force Academy on the basis of academic failure. Roy, after much effort, finished a degree at another university. He found adequate work but continued to struggle with regret and lack of fulfillment. With much effort, Daniel also went on to finish a university degree and settled into a successful career. Both were aware of God's hand on their lives. Both learned valuable lessons in their failures.

We have met the enemy and it is us. — Simple
J. Malarkey, in the comic strip *Pogo*

IMPACT AND CONSEQUENCES

When our work lives get put on hold for whatever reason, we enter difficult and unknown territory. The consequences reach deeply into our personal lives and families. Strains and disruptions can result in three different areas:

1. Financial. The financial impact can be devastating. Savings vanish, homes are lost, and bankruptcy becomes a possibility. Unemployment compensation certainly helps but is rarely adequate. Bills go unpaid. Every dollar is used for necessities.

2. Emotional. Many people experience discouragement leading to depression. Crushed egos give way to fear, anger, and conflict. Some people are embarrassed by their situation and withdraw from friends and family. Isolation results. This was the case with some friends in our church who lost their jobs. After the husband lost his job, we rarely saw them. They found it too hard to keep responding to questions about finding employment. Soon they felt it was easier to stay home and watch TV.

3. Spiritual. The spiritual impact of a work crisis can either drive us toward God or further away from Him. We may question Him: *Where is God? Does He hear my prayers? Doesn't He care?* We may question ourselves: *What have I done wrong? Did I work hard enough? Do I really have a future with fulfilling work?*

So how do you deal with those aspects of your career that are unfinished? How can you move beyond your regrets and work to avoid more regret in the future? The answer, in part, begins with your perspective and your theology. Let's take a look at both of these.

A MATTER OF PERSPECTIVE

When unemployment in the U.S. reached 10 percent, meaning that every tenth person was out of work, the impact was pervasive. Many men and women were working in jobs that did not satisfy them or tap their potential. Yet in the developing world, 10 percent unemployment would be cause for rejoicing. In many countries, 15, 20, 30 percent—and even higher percentages—of the people are out of work, some never finding a job that supports their family. Few people have choices in finding work that satisfies. That is a privilege in the minority Western world that is easy to overlook. It helps to remember the extent of our blessings compared to much of the world. It can give us a measure of perspective as we process our circumstances under God's leading.

Jerry's stepfather is a good example of a person who did not have the career he wanted but who found satisfaction in being employed and supporting his family. Unable to get the basic business education he wanted, he ended up working as a truck driver in the freight business for his entire life. He worked hard. Even though his career dreams were never realized, he never complained. He was happy to have a job. After he retired, he put his experience to use as an adjuster for damaged freight, coincidentally, for a company called Jerry White and Associates. His work was honorable. He worked hard, lifting and moving freight on the dock alongside twenty-five-year-olds when he was in his sixties. He became a model of a man who did what he needed to do. He understood that work and career do not comprise the totality of life and that family, marriage, and health form equally important facets of life.

The issue of perspective can also be instructive for women who have served most of their lives as homemakers and mothers, particularly if these were not the careers they dreamed of having. Women who spend years being educated and trained often want to put their skills and talents to use in the public marketplace, yet they never get the opportunity to do so. It can help to remember that a career as a homemaker is a noble and fulfilling career. Don't lose sight of this perspective.

Our ability to deal well with regrets and crises in our work lives also has to do with our theology.

AN ISSUE OF THEOLOGY

Theology? You've got to be kidding! What has theology got to do with an unfinished career? Almost everything. How we view life and work biblically determines how we respond to work that is less than satisfying. A biblical view of success also forms how we respond when our careers fall short of our vision and dreams.

It is not the purpose of this book to develop a full theology of work, but here are a few key truths that can help you respond well to the unfinished aspects of career and work:

- **All work is sacred.** There is no separation between secular work and work as a professional in church or Christian organizations. All work is a divine plan of God. No matter the job, we are working for and with Him.
- **From the beginning of history, God honored work and the worker.** He ordained work for man before he fell into that fateful first sin. "The LORD God took the man and put him in the Garden of Eden to work it and take care of it."[1]
- **Work became more difficult as a result of the Fall.** "Cursed is the ground because of you; through painful toil you will eat of it all the days of your life. It will produce thorns and thistles for you, and you will eat the plants of the field. By the sweat of your brow you will eat your food until you return to the ground, since from it you were taken; for dust you are and to dust you will return."[2]

- **Adam's sin did not degrade the value and meaning of work.** When God commanded Moses to build the tabernacle, He did not tell him to get the cheapest, most incompetent workers. He told him to choose workers with great skill in every area of work needed. "Tell all the skilled men to whom I have given wisdom in such matters that they are to make garments for Aaron, for his consecration, so he may serve me as priest."[3]

  When Daniel was carried captive into Babylon, God gave him great skill and wisdom. "To these four young men God gave knowledge and understanding of all kinds of literature and learning. And Daniel could understand visions and dreams of all kinds."[4]

  Jesus worked as a carpenter with His father until He reached the age of thirty. His disciples were all ordinary workers, common people.

- **God ordained work for pleasure, creativity, and provision.** Our work does not just provide for our finances; it allows us to participate in God's plan for us. Enjoy it!

- **There is honor and dignity in all types of work.** Financial remuneration is not a measure of one's worth or work value, and there is no difference in value between types of work (for instance, truck drivers, managers, doctors, engineers, construction workers, sales clerks). In the Old Testament, Joseph distinguished himself as a servant, slave, and trustee in a prison before he became the prime minister of Egypt. He did what he needed to do, not just what he liked to do. He was faithful to his masters, from slave owner to prison warden to pharaoh. He did his work well because he feared God and served Him.

- **No one has a "right" to work in a job that always fits his or her gifting.**

- **Life fulfillment does not come solely from work or career, yet fulfillment in work is valid and good.**

- **God blesses both the wealthy and the poor with contentment.**

RETHINKING THE FUTURE

As much as you might like, you cannot turn the clock back and redo decisions you made or undo events that happened in your work life. You can not change history, nor can you easily change who you are. God gave you your unique talents, personality, and life circumstances. You are the person He made you to be. If basic mathematics always came hard for you, most likely you will not develop into an engineer.

Your inability to change the past doesn't mean you should give up or be fatalistic, however, because there are many skills and abilities you can develop. You can learn from your mistakes and poor decisions. You can plot a new path. You can begin to move forward, whether your setback came from adverse circumstances, poor choices, or ill health.

The first step in rethinking your career future is a realistic assessment of what brought you to this point. Determine the reasons you aren't where you thought you would be or wanted to be. Don't offer excuses. Write out a description of the circumstances that contributed to your current situation. Be specific: unemployment, inadequate pay, job dissatisfaction, a forced move, illness. Then consider the following ways to enhance your job opportunities:

- Get more education or training. Increase your skills in your current work or become qualified in another skill. Take advantage of any training your company offers.
- Be willing to work part-time to gain another skill.
- Work hard at the job you have, whatever it is.
- If necessary, downsize your lifestyle to further your future.

SUBMIT TO HIS PLAN

Career setbacks are God's detours. He has our best interests at heart.

Gary Nelson (Jerry's cousin) is learning this firsthand. He worked as a key person in the cooperative feed and grain business in Garden City, Iowa. He knew every aspect of the business, dealing with the farmers in the community. One day he was helping unload a railroad freight car. As he walked along the roof of the car, someone accidentally bumped him. He fell to the ground, shattering his feet and ankles. He was suddenly thrust into a world of surgery, pain, therapy, discouragement, and financial realities. After many surgeries, he found it impossible to take up his work responsibilities again. He also had to ponder the why of the accident as well as God's plan for him now.

Gary is in the middle of an unfinished career, but he is trusting in the truth that God is sovereign over every aspect of our lives, so he's submitting to His plan for redirecting his life and career.

God does provide. We do not need to worry or be anxious about our work lives. He wants us to seek Him first and place our trust in Him. He can finish what is unfinished.

QUESTIONS FOR REFLECTION

1. What is "unfinished" about your work or career?
2. Identify some of the causes of it being unfinished.
3. How do you think about your work? Do you see it as a necessity? A blessing? A calling? A burden? A _____?
4. What steps can you take now to move into the next stage of your career and work?

CHAPTER 6

UNFINISHED RELATIONSHIPS

You can't antagonize and influence at the same time.

UNKNOWN

L ee was the eldest of several children in a family who farmed, very successfully, in the Midwest. Lee's father was demanding of him in both farmwork and social development. When Lee disappointed his father, there were always severe consequences. His father beat him and criticized him sharply. Lee's mother often tried to intervene, but her pleas were ignored.

As soon as he graduated from high school, Lee joined the army and never spoke to his father again. Occasionally, he would reach out to his mother or one of his siblings, but their conversations always ended with bitter words and further separation. He married but never had children. Anger and resentment defined his life and poisoned his relationships. Lee lived into his nineties. He died old, alone, and harboring hostility, even toward people who wanted to love and care for him in his old age.

What a sad portrait of a life with unfinished relationships! Here is another.

Robert Louis Stevenson told the story of two maiden sisters in Edinburgh. The sisters lived comfortably in a rather large one-room apartment, but one day they had a disagreement. As time passed, their anger grew and they stopped speaking to each other. Instead of resolving

65

their dispute or one of them moving out, they both stubbornly stayed in the apartment, all the while refusing to communicate. According to Stevenson,

> *A chalk line drawn upon the floor separated their two domains; it bisected the doorway and the fireplace, so that each could go out and in and do her cooking without violating the territory of the other. So, for years, they coexisted in a hateful silence. . . . In the dark watches, each could hear the breathing of her enemy. Never did four walls look down upon an uglier spectacle.*[1]

What happened? How did these people end up with such fractured relationships?

WHY MOST RELATIONSHIPS GET BROKEN

Most of us don't start out being unforgiving. Little children often squabble and holler at one another, "I never want to see you again," but thirty minutes later they are playing together peacefully. Adults could take a lesson from this pattern.

Sadly, as children reach their teens, their disagreements escalate and forgiveness comes hard. We have all seen TV depictions of teens bullying each other, calling one another by vicious names, spreading lies, pushing and shoving, and sometimes even trying to murder a perceived enemy. By the time we reach adulthood, the more obvious forms of retaliation diminish. Instead, we harbor resentment that leads us to strike back in more subtle ways, usually through harsh, accusatory words and failure to forgive. Relationships break under such treatment. Most unfinished relationships are due to arguments, misunderstandings, and strong disagreements.

The book of Acts tells the story of how two men in ministry together had a sharp disagreement that broke the relationship. Paul and Barnabas ministered and traveled and suffered together for the cause of the gospel. They had the same theology, the same enthusiasm for serving God, the same tolerance for a truly difficult lifestyle. But they disagreed over a seemingly small issue, and the argument grew so heated that they parted ways.

Some time later Paul said to Barnabas, "Let us go back and visit the brothers in all the towns where we preached the word of the Lord and see how they are doing." Barnabas wanted to take John, also called Mark, with them, but Paul did not think it wise to take him, because he had deserted them in Pamphylia and had not continued with them in the work. They had such a sharp disagreement that they parted company. Barnabas took Mark and sailed for Cyprus, but Paul chose Silas and left, commended by the brothers to the grace of the Lord.[2]

This story describes how a seemingly small decision can escalate into a "sharp disagreement" and lead to a broken relationship. Although both Paul and Silas continued serving the Lord and carrying the gospel, one can only imagine the sorrow they felt at their parting, each feeling misunderstood and frustrated. They no doubt spent hours regretting the breach in their friendship and rationalizing their own positions. How strongly they must have regretted the harsh words that brought an end to their long service together.

If arguments, misunderstandings, and disagreements are the cause of most broken relationships, shouldn't we do our best to avoid such things? What can we do?

THE BEST WAY TO AVOID A POTENTIAL BREAK

One of the best ways to defuse an impending argument or even a full-blown fight is to use the statement "You may be right." This gives both parties some leeway and brings a breathing space that can allow tempers to cool and reason to return. This statement leaves both people with some dignity and self-respect and brings an abrupt close to the argument.

A soft answer turns away wrath, but grievous words stir up anger. — Proverbs 15:1 (AMP)

Loud voices and cruel words never persuade; they only alienate. Defusing disagreements as quickly as possible is one of the best ways to preserve treasured relationships. But even if a relationship gets broken, reconciliation is possible.

RECONCILING BROKEN RELATIONSHIPS

Bob, Ray, and Mike were three brothers who went into a technology business together in their twenties. The business was wildly successful and the money poured in. They considered the work as much a ministry as a true business. They influenced many people to come to faith, and their company was held as an ideal model in their community.

As technology developed and expanded, Ray and Mike wanted to invest heavily in new fields. Bob, much more fiscally conservative, held back reluctantly. Ray and Mike continued to cajole, plead, and finally demand that Bob release the funds to enlarge the business. Bob responded with frustration and anger, yelling at his brothers, even cursing at them, before storming away from the building.

Ray and Mike, holding the majority of the stock and having convinced the board, went ahead with their plans. Bob refused to come to work or even speak to his brothers. This breach affected not just their business but also their families and their church, where the three brothers served in significant leadership positions. Even the wider community began to speculate and review what had happened to cause such a rift in this family.

About a year later, the business began to experience significant financial difficulty and the stock market sagged. Ray and Mike, the creative geniuses of the company, realized they had seriously miscalculated the expansion. After talking it over, they realized that Bob's stability and fiscal conservatism had kept the company on an even financial keel. They asked to meet with him but wisely understood that they couldn't just ask him to return and rescue the company. They knew they had to ask forgiveness for their impetuous insistence on expansion and their treatment of Bob.

When the three brothers met in Ray's home, Bob was eager to forgive them. He in turn asked Mike and Ray to forgive him for abandoning the business and viewing his brothers with anger and bitterness. Tears flowed and they ended their conversation with brotherly hugs and prayer.

What can we learn from this story about reconciling a broken relationship?

- Broken relationships never exist in a vacuum. Waves of trouble ripple out from the original problem and affect many other people.
- Delayed forgiveness and resolution to broken relationships hardens into bitterness and makes the conflict more difficult to resolve.
- When ego is set aside, someone takes the first step and forgiveness rules.

The writer of Hebrews knew the devastation that unfinished relationships would cause in the lives of the early Christians and offers this remedy: "Make every effort to live in peace with all men and to be holy; without holiness no one will see the Lord. See to it that no one misses the grace of God and that no bitter root grows up to cause trouble and defile many."[3]

Oh, that can be challenging to do! Have you ever spent wakeful hours in bed at night, reviewing a conversation with someone who has offended or accused you? During those imaginary talks, we always find just the right thing to respond with—that "zinger" that will set the other person straight. But these kinds of useless speculations never bring healing or restoration. In fact, they might even escalate the problem, causing our attempts at reconciliation to be met with rejection.

God describes the appropriate action to take: "Bear with each other and forgive whatever grievances you may have against one another. Forgive as the Lord forgave you."[4] Pretty clear, isn't it? This advice—command, really—is repeated in many other areas of the Gospels and Epistles.

It boils down to this: What's the best way to prevent and restore broken relationships? Practice *tolerance* and *forgiveness*, two Holy Spirit–given keys.

Everyone has idiosyncrasies and failures. Some people are even downright evil. But God loves them as much as He loves us, and He insists that we show tolerance to everyone. He also commands that we forgive all the complaints we have against others. Even when there's injustice, unfairness, and downright evil? Yes, because forgiveness is more about the forgiver than the forgiven. When we fail to forgive even the most grievous offenses, we are held captive to the offender—to resentment, anger, and bitterness against that person.

One of the most alarming passages in Scripture tells us that if we fail to forgive, God will not forgive us: "If you forgive men when they sin against you, your heavenly Father will also forgive you. But if you do not forgive men their sins, your Father will not forgive your sins."[5]

Are you living with unfinished relationships that are broken? Are there steps to take today to bring healing and reconciliation? Someone has said that the six most powerful words in relationships are *"I was wrong. Please forgive me."* These words can bring closure and healing to many broken and unfinished relationships. Is there someone you need to say them to today?

QUESTIONS FOR REFLECTION

1. What makes broken relationships difficult to restore?
2. Are there specific relationships that remain unresolved and unfinished for you? Which ones?
3. What biblical principles can you apply to your relationships to restore or build them?
4. Discuss why it may be necessary to leave some relationships unfinished.

CHAPTER 7

UNFINISHED SPIRITUALITY

If you only get the foundation laid and then run out of money, you're going to look pretty foolish. Everyone passing by will poke fun at you: "He started something he couldn't finish."

LUKE 14:29-30 (MSG)

Consider the following possible responses to the question "Are you a spiritual person?"

- "A spiritual person? Of course I am. I have deep feelings. I love nature. I care for people. I believe in God."
- "I'm not sure. Probably not. I'm not Mother Teresa. I'm more like John Lennon. He was spiritual, wasn't he?"
- "Probably not. I believe in Jesus. And God. But I do so many dumb things. I get angry. I have a lot of lust. Spiritual? I don't think I'll ever get there."
- "Of course. I go to church. I even spoke in tongues once. I like the feeling of being close to God. But that doesn't happen very often."
- "Spiritual? Yes. Doesn't the Bible say we are all spiritual beings? I really feel things. Sometimes I feel close to God. Other times I feel as though God has slammed the door in my face because

I'm not worthy. I have so much shame. So maybe I am
unspiritual."

- "I'm born again. I know I will go to heaven. So I must be
spiritual, right?"
- "I'm really working on being more spiritual. I read my Bible
almost every day. I pray. I read books on spirituality and holy
living. Am I spiritual enough? Heavens, no. I've got a long way
to go. But I work hard at it."
- "Who cares? Dumb question."
- "Well, I heard the saying 'God is not through with me yet.' So
I guess I am a work in progress. But does that make me
spiritual? I think so. I hope so."

At one time or another in their lives, most people have cycled
through several of these ideas of spirituality. The two of us believe that
everyone, and especially the follower of Christ, wants to be spiritual.

It's also true that most people eventually look back on life with
some regrets. Few would say they had attained the peak of spiritual
maturity. Most Christians would admit that they could do more for the
kingdom and could grow more spiritually—that their spiritual lives are
unfinished. Why is that so often the case, and can we do anything about
it? What, if anything, can we finish in our spiritual lives?

Before we explore these questions, let's take a look at what things
have already been finished in our spiritual lives and what things can
never be finished.

WHAT HAS ALREADY BEEN FINISHED?

Some aspects of our spirituality are already complete. Our sins—past,
present, and future—are forgiven. Our pardon for sin, new birth, and
salvation is secure. There is nothing more to be done in these areas.

When Jesus announced on the cross, "It is finished,"[1] He declared
that He had finished what He had come to do: die for the sins of

all, finally and for all time. *The Message* says,

> *As a priest, Christ made a single sacrifice for sins, and that was it! Then he sat down right beside God and waited for his enemies to cave in. It was a perfect sacrifice by a perfect person to perfect some very imperfect people. By that single offering, he did everything that needed to be done for everyone who takes part in the purifying process.*[2]

Jesus' death on the cross secured our pardon for sin and fulfilled all the requirements needed to make our new birth and personal salvation complete. There is nothing we can do to earn salvation, nor do we need to fear that we might lose it. Our forgiveness is complete. We cannot sin our way out of God's family. The Holy Spirit resides in us permanently to help us live and grow as believers: "You also were included in Christ when you heard the word of truth, the gospel of your salvation. Having believed, you were marked in him with a seal, the promised Holy Spirit."[3]

WHAT IS NEVER FINISHED?

What is never finished, at least while we are on this earth? Our spiritual growth. Our walk with God. Our daily victory over sin. Our knowledge of God. So it is not necessarily a concern if our spirituality is unfinished. However, it is a concern if the reason our spirituality is unfinished is that we have simply stopped growing—or never started at all.

WHAT CAN BE FINISHED?

We don't have to wait to get to heaven to be spiritually mature; we can reach significant spiritual maturity here on earth. This requires that we continue growing and surrendering control of our lives to God.

But even though spiritual maturity is possible for each believer, many don't reach it. They stop growing. This is a pervasive problem among Christians, so let's explore why this is the case and what can be done about it.

WHY SOME CHRISTIANS STOP GROWING

Sadly, many Christians live in a "Let George do it" world, leaving the religious pursuits to a few chosen professional Christians or laypeople who are somehow known as spiritually inclined people. That is a fallacy implanted early in our lives.

Jerry's wonderful grandmother felt concerned as she saw him getting more and more involved in aspects of Christianity. She was pleased, but she warned, "Don't get too radical." The view that "a little spirituality is good, but don't go too far" permeates the thinking of many Christians. That leads to an innocuous and sterile Christianity that says, "Go to church, sometimes. Be a believer, certainly. Be moral and marry a moral spouse. Inoculate yourself against some mysterious retribution from God. Be good but not too good. Be 'safely' spiritual or religious. Be moderately convicted but not so much so that it affects your pleasure or your quest for monetary and materialistic goals."

This view is not only nonsense, it is dangerous nonsense. It stunts our growth and makes "believers" absolutely ineffective in changing the world, reducing the divorce rate, changing the moral direction of our country, and modeling commitment to their children, the next generation.

Another reason Christians don't grow into spiritual maturity is that they are left to fend for themselves while still in the infant stage of their growth. Spiritual growth is a process that begins with a profound decision to allow the Lordship of Jesus Christ to be the controlling element in our lives. When we become believers, we lay our spiritual foundation—and we often grow like mad in some of the fundamentals of faith. Like babies, we are hungry for spiritual nourishment. We seek out spiritual fellowship and begin reading and taking the Bible seriously. But, also like babies, we are too young to know how to feed ourselves.

Too often what happens to a new believer is similar to what would happen if an infant were brought home from the hospital, pointed to the kitchen, and told, "Welcome home. The food is all there. Go get it. Eat all you want." It sounds ridiculous, but, in essence, that is what happens to many new believers. Without the proper spiritual nourishment, they stop growing. Their condition is described in the book of Hebrews:

> *Though by this time you ought to be teachers, you need someone to teach you the elementary truths of God's word all over again. You need milk, not solid food! Anyone who lives on milk, being still an infant, is not acquainted with the teaching about righteousness. But solid food is for the mature, who by constant use have trained themselves to distinguish good from evil.*[4]

This passage is a picture of stunted growth. When our physical growth is stunted, it's obvious. Not so with our spiritual growth; it is much more subtle. People simply stop growing without being aware of it. They become complacent and satisfied spiritually and fearful of changes that they perceive to be demanding or difficult.

This is compounded by the fact that many Christians have only a vague idea of where they are in their spiritual growth. When asked, "Are you satisfied with your spirituality or spiritual growth?" most will acknowledge that they are not but, as we saw in the opening comments, have difficulty answering what that means. They don't even know if they are growing.

It doesn't have to be that way.[5]

HOW TO KNOW IF YOU ARE GROWING

Scripture gives us some important indicators of spirituality and spiritual maturity. Their presence in a person points to continued spiritual growth. Here are a few indicators:

Assurance of conversion. One cannot spiritually grow until the seed of faith has been firmly planted. To mature, a person needs clear assurance that he or she is a follower of Jesus and has received His forgiveness and salvation. This is critical because doubting one's salvation cripples any substantial growth.

Do not confuse ritualistic religious events such as infant or adult baptism, confirmation, and church membership with true conversion. Conversion is *personal*, a matter between you and God. It is an issue of true belief, not words of a prayer.[6]

Conversion can occur in the heart before any specific prayer or public action occurs, or it can follow those actions. What matters is assurance of salvation, not a memory of the precise moment of salvation. Mary was raised in a Christian home and cannot remember a time when she made that first commitment, but she has a steadfast assurance of her relationship with Christ. Her heart is firm on the matter. Jerry, on the other hand, has a strong memory of his prayer to receive Christ. He had been considering the facts of the gospel for some time and prayed to receive Christ while sitting in a car with a college student who was helping in a summer youth program. Jerry knew that a key transaction had taken place and immediately told his parents. Even so, for some time, he prayed every night to receive Christ, wondering if his conversion really "took."

Doubts are not unusual for a younger person, or even adults. It seems so simple that one can pray and in that moment be assured of eternal life, yet that is the profound teaching of Scripture.[7]

Active fellowship with other believers. Many people who claim to be Christians have little or no connection with other believers, yet no one survives alone spiritually. If you avoid contact and connection with other believers, it is a clear sign of spiritual immaturity.

The author of Hebrews wrote, "Let us not give up meeting together, as some are in the habit of doing, but let us encourage one another—and all the more as you see the Day approaching."[8] In his letter to the Romans, Paul said, "I remember you in my prayers at all times; and I pray that now at last by God's will the way may be opened for me to come to you. I long to see you so that I may impart to you some spiritual gift to make you strong—that is, that you and I may be mutually encouraged by each other's faith."[9] Paul saw the necessity of personal contact with the other believers.

Christians who are growing are actively involved in a local church or some significant fellowship of believers. The definitions of *church* and *church attendance* are not as pronounced as they once were, which is why we say you need to be involved with a "group of believers" who are encouraging you to grow spiritually. Many people, after being part of a church for a while, experience difficult problems. They see believers fighting and disparaging their leaders and each other. They see pastors sin and leave the ministry. They see hypocrisy at its height. Consequently, they reject the organized church, and many stop meeting with other believers altogether.

What should you do when you encounter situations such as these in a church? Never give up on meeting with other Christians. Focus on finding a group of believers that feeds you and your children well, and stick with it. Participate in a small-group Bible study at your church or among your friends. Whatever it takes, seek out fellowship.

Regular Scripture reading and prayer. A believer can't survive without these disciplines. They are basic. Having a daily devotional time is like eating a meal. It takes food to grow, and the Word and prayer are spiritual food.

Just read the Bible for ten or fifteen minutes in the morning, or whenever you can, on a regular basis. There are a number of good Bible-reading plans available. If you are unsure of where to begin reading, start in the New Testament in the gospel of Mark. Don't start in Leviticus!

Pray for your family, the day, friends, and special needs. Thank God for your blessings. For help in establishing a daily devotional time, we suggest Ruth Myers' *How to Have a Quiet Time* and Robert Foster's *7 Minutes with God*.[10]

Changes in character. When Mary plants seeds in our garden (not

Jerry's forte), she looks for the new growth in the next days. If she sees none, she knows there is no life in the plant.

Each of us needs to make a similar kind of assessment regarding changes in our character. Ask yourself, *Am I becoming more like Christ? Am I different—kinder, gentler, more patient, more loving—than I was a year ago? How do I know? What am I doing to maintain my growth? What evidence does my spouse, friends, or children see?*

Character may be the deepest and most elusive mark of spiritual maturity. Even the definition of "good character" involves many facets. Certainly it includes many of the virtues: honesty, integrity, kindness, compassion, gentleness, and love. Paul tells us, "The fruit of the Spirit is love, joy, peace, patience, kindness, goodness, faithfulness, gentleness and self-control. Against such things there is no law."[11] These Christian virtues are strong indicators of good character.

Which ones are present in your life? Make your own list. How are you growing in each virtue?

Not only should your character be shaped by the fruits of the Spirit but it should also be centered on Christ. Jesus reflected and perfected these virtues. Outside of a life with Him, you will not be able to truly deepen spiritually. It is Jesus first, now and always. If at the center of your life you do not find Him, then you lack the only part of maturity that counts. If He is at the center, He controls your life and the decisions you make. You are obeying the Scriptures and praying on a daily basis, seeking His guidance. Paul describes this in Colossians 3:1-4.

Spiritually speaking, yesterday's meal will not sustain you for the week ahead. To grow, you must surrender to God in a way that affects how you live. You need to be obedient to what you read in Scripture and see your life change.

GROWING INTO SPIRITUAL MATURITY

If you want to become spiritually mature, you need short-term and long-term spiritual goals. For the short-term goals, commit to a daily time with God—reading, reflecting, and praying. The GROWING IN CHRIST Bible studies and the LIFECHANGE Bible studies are great resources. These habits and this growth must become part of our life patterns. They form the foundation of spiritual growth. For the long-term goals, begin planning goals for strengthening your marriage, deveoping your view of work, being a better parent or grandparent, and deepening your knowledge of biblical and spiritual matters.

At the four-year point in our marriage, we encountered significant conflict and difficulty. We had to reorder our priorities, especially regarding Jerry's pace and work schedule. He worked such long hours that days would pass when he wouldn't see our son, much less spend time with Mary. Learning new patterns for marriage was a significant part of our spiritual growth. Since then, we have sought help from others. We have even sought counseling (not to fix our marriage but to develop it).

We also began an extensive study of parenting and grandparenting. We found there was much we should or could have done but also much we could do in the future. Some of these decisions are in our book *When Your Kids Aren't Kids Anymore*.[12]

You can keep growing in all areas of life. You can develop into a spiritually mature person.

START NOW!

You can't finish what you have not yet started. You can't redo the foolishness of sin and the seasons of a lack of commitment. You can't lead your family spiritually when your children are grown and no longer live in your home or when your marriage has ended. You can't replay the past and do it differently.

Jerry recently met with a successful businessman who wanted to use his skills in some kind of ministry context. During the conversation, Jerry quoted a couple of Bible verses and the man asked, "How did you know those verses?" He wanted very much to serve God. He was serious about his spiritual life, but he had not built a foundation biblically or in his personal growth. To grow and mature, we have to know the basics; otherwise, we are like a salesperson who is motivated and enthusiastic but lacks sufficient knowledge of the product he or she is selling.

In one of our first Air Force assignments, we visited a church in town. The pastor then visited us. He flipped easily through the Bible, telling us we needed to do certain things to be assured of our salvation. Jerry told him, "I know you are wrong, but I'm not sure just where it is in the Bible." That experience made us resolve to study the Scriptures for ourselves and not just rely on what we had heard or been taught.

No, you can't finish what you haven't even started, but you can start your spiritual journey right now.

If you are unsure of your salvation, take time now to pray and commit your past, your sins, and your life to Jesus Christ. *Lord, I confess You now as my Lord and Savior. Please come into my life and begin to make me into the person You want me to be.*

If you are already a follower of Jesus, renew your commitment to grow spiritually. You can begin every day with a time with God. You can finish each day living out His life in your work and home. You can set and complete goals of personal and spiritual growth. You can know that when you come to the end of your life that you have finished the work He gave you to do. Jesus did. Paul did. So can you.

QUESTIONS FOR REFLECTION

1. Discuss and describe what *spirituality* means to you.
2. How would you respond if asked, "Are you a spiritual person?"
3. What aspects of spirituality will remain unfinished?
4. What areas of your spiritual walk need to be finished or built up?

From the movie *An Unfinished Life*:

Mitch Bradley (Morgan Freeman): "Would you bury me next to Griffin?"

Einar Gilkyson (Robert Redford): "Don't you think you oughta die first?"

Einar Gilkyson: "My son is dead."

Mitch Bradley: "Your granddaughter's not, and neither are you."

CHAPTER 8

UNFINISHED LIVES

In 1818 Franz Schubert was in the midst of his greatest work when suddenly he died. But today the world still stands in reverence and adoration when the violins and the organ and the harps and the flutes play The Unfinished Symphony!

L. D. NEWTON

After four years in the Air Force, we were transferred from Cape Kennedy in Florida to Dayton, Ohio. As is customary, the Air Force arranged to pack and move our household goods to our new home. When we arrived in Dayton, we called for the delivery of our goods from the warehouse where they had been stored while we made the trip to our new location. A warehouse employee said, "We're so sorry to have to tell you this, but the warehouse burned down." We had been told this was a fireproof warehouse!

We decided to see for ourselves. Indeed, the warehouse was still standing, more or less, as it was constructed of cement cinderblock. But the contents, the possessions of twenty-eight military families, were totally destroyed and laid in smoldering, blackened heaps on the floor.

Did this event change our lives? Undoubtedly. For months, we spent hours replacing baby clothes, furniture, kitchen implements, clothes, and all sorts of miscellanea. Memorabilia, photos, wedding mementos were lost forever. But now, as we look back on this event, it is but a minor blip in our lives; it has very little significance. The loss of our earthly possessions taught us a valuable lesson. We are reminded of these words from Jesus: "A man's life does not consist in the abundance of his possessions."[1]

Events that carry lasting significance involve not things but people. These events can be instantaneous, such as a stroke, traumatic injury, or stock market crash. Or they can develop over time: a deteriorating marriage, a progressive illness, the debilitating effects of aging, the foreclosure on a cherished home. Experiences like these often leave people feeling that their lives are destroyed and unfinished.

Can catastrophic events lead to an unfinished life? Sadly, yes. Some people never recover from overwhelming conditions in their lives; they are forever caught in a cycle of despair and anger and bitterness, questioning the goodness of God. But others fight their way back with God's help to a place of acceptance and peace, living with the difficult circumstances that have impacted their lives. What makes the difference? How can you find peace?

FINDING PEACE AND ACCEPTANCE DESPITE TRAUMATIC EVENTS

When life events impact us in ways that leave us reeling and broken, there are ways to find peace and acceptance.

Allow God to use the event to redirect and transform. Great potential can follow overwhelming events. Our lives are not "over" when something horrible happens. They are redirected, changed. When traumatic events interrupt our lives, we must look to God for a new life, new relationships, new dreams.

Our friend Ken contracted polio between his junior and senior years of high school. This happened during the terrible scourge of polio before Jonas Salk developed life-saving vaccines. People went into virtual self-imposed quarantine to avoid the disease. During that long summer, parents kept their children at home, church services were canceled, and movie theaters remained shuttered. Families made only brief trips to purchase groceries or conduct essential business.

But the epidemic raged on and Ken succumbed. He survived in an iron lung, captive to the mechanical contraption that kept his lungs functioning. Eventually, he used more portable equipment that allowed him some freedom, but he spent his life in a wheelchair, dependent on others for his care and sustenance. Was Ken's life unfinished in that he lived with unrealized dreams and ambitions? The answer is an unqualified yes. But despite these unfinished aspects of his life, he adjusted, created new dreams, and lived a productive and content life.

Moses did something similar. In Genesis, we read his life story. For forty years, he lived in luxury and privilege in Pharaoh's palace in Egypt. After murdering an Egyptian (justly, he thought), he fled to the desert to hide. He spent another forty years there living a dramatically different lifestyle. He became a shepherd, married, had children, and experienced amazing encounters with God.[2] All of his experiences in the desert prepared him for the final years of his life, when he became a national leader, a spiritual director, and a conduit for God's direct revelation to the nation of Israel.

Lean on trusted friends and family for support. Times of difficulty and weakness can lead to anger, embarrassment, resentment, and feeling misunderstood. We don't always want others to know of our situations. We feel they won't appreciate or understand the depth of our suffering. But trusted friends and family provide essential support and encourage us to trust God to bring us through the trauma and open new vistas and opportunities to live life to its fullest.

Marion had always been an industrious, fun-loving individual, active in her church and community. She was observant of others and quick to meet needs and help in any way. People often commented on how much she could accomplish in a day. Her home was organized and spotless, her children were happy, her husband admired her, and her friends and fellow church members relied on her for help in myriad activities.

One day as she sat at her sewing machine quilting for a missions project, she started crying and couldn't stop. For the next few weeks, she wept every day, hiding her sadness from her family and friends. Then her husband arrived home early from work one afternoon and found her crying. Consultations with medical doctors, counselors, and psychiatrists finally revealed that she carried a low-grade infection in her system that left her weary and depressed. During the years of her long recovery, she found faithful friends who walked along with her. Others, who had simply been using her for her abilities and helpfulness, disappeared. She learned the truth of an old proverb, "A friend loves at all times."[3]

One friend, especially, supported Marion fully. She understood the pressure Marion was feeling and stood by her, often defending her against people who were disappointed that Marion was no longer serving them and their needs. She wiped Marion's tears, prayed with her, listened as Marion expressed her discouragement, then listened again and yet again. The friend's patient listening was a gift that allowed Marion to express herself. Love and acceptance by her faithful friend aided her healing as much as medication and professional advice. Part of her recovery was learning that she had high value as a person, not for what she could do but for who she was. This led to a strong inner peace and faith that sustained her for years.

Harrowing, traumatic changes in life can be overcome; great accomplishments can follow overwhelming events if we allow God to use them to redirect and change us. In all of these circumstances, He is waiting for us to turn to Him for perspective, healing, strength, and grace to endure.

FINDING PEACE AND ACCEPTANCE WHEN A LIFE IS TAKEN TOO SOON

Our son, Steve, was brutally and senselessly murdered on his job when he was thirty years old. He had offended no one; he didn't deserve to have his life taken by a killer. He was an innocent victim of a brutal murderer.

Steve was a caring and sensitive man who went out of his way to serve and help others. A hard worker, he held two jobs. He was a radio announcer for our local National Public Radio station, and he also owned and drove a cab. One fateful night, a taxi fare shot him three times in the back of the head, killing him instantly. This terrible act led to years of trauma, suffering, and grief for our family and Steve's wife, Julie. There were years of legal proceedings that finally resulted in the killer's being sentenced to prison for a lengthy term.

Was Steve's life unfinished? Yes, in that he had dreams and goals he was unable to finish. Our lives are unfinished as well. Our hopes and aspirations for our son died with him, and an empty place remained. Only Steve, no one else, could fill that place.

But God's plans for Steve were finished. The psalmist declares that "all the days ordained for me were written in your book before one of them came to be."[4] From God's vantage point, Steve's life was not cut short; it was complete. Romans 8:28 reassures us that God has only our good in mind: "We know that in all things God works for the good of those who love him, who have been called according to his purpose." God's Word is true. The love and grace of God covers any difficulty or suffering we might encounter in life.

Others we know have experienced this same supernatural peace in the midst of the seemingly premature loss of a loved one. Andy and Ellie eagerly awaited the arrival of their first child. When he was born, their son was a beautiful, big baby with lots of dark hair and chubby cheeks, but he never opened his eyes or cried. In spite of the frantic efforts of medical personnel, two minutes after their son was born, he stopped breathing.

The death of their much-anticipated baby left Andy and Ellie with an empty nursery and breaking hearts. Even though they had three healthy, living children born to them over the next seven years, Andy and Ellie continued to quietly mourn the loss of their firstborn. Eighteen years later, Ellie said, "A day never goes by that I don't think of him and wonder what he would be now—graduating from high school, getting ready for college—maybe an athlete, maybe an artist. We will never forget him."

Although they continue to grieve their loss, Andy and Ellie have found peace and acceptance by deepening their faith in God's goodness and choosing to focus on the rich blessings God brought into their lives.

The Old Testament records the death of King David's baby son.[5] The baby, born as a result of David's adultery with Bathsheba, became ill. Desperate, David pleaded with God for the baby's life, again and again asking Him to let his son live. But the baby died. The Scripture says that "the LORD struck the child." This story troubles us as we ponder the reason that little life was so short. David's life changed forever as he contemplated the unfinished life of his baby son.

Life can change in an instant. Tragic events such as these direct our thoughts to the value of life, the insignificance of possessions, and the worth of deep relationships. Knowing how quickly the direction of life can change helps us remember to focus on the important things. God's gifts to us are His love, His Spirit, His Word, and relationships with people. Other things are secondary and fleeting.

Although we should always be alert to this momentous truth, when life is simple and easy, we are inclined to forget our most basic priorities. Daily reading of Scripture, prayer, and fellowship with other believers help wounded people keep their focus on the true values of life and a relationship with God.

LINGERING QUESTIONS

God determines how long we will live. Our lives are finished when *He* says they are finished. He knows the events that shape and change our lives. He alone controls the universe and each individual life. But even when our faith in God's sovereignty is strong, questions linger and perplex us: *Why do these difficult things happen? Why do some people suffer more than others? How can we determine some good from these terrible events?*

Dan Foster, a gifted musician, wrote a song that speaks directly to these questions:

> *I don't understand why some people must suffer*
> *Or why children and young people die.*
> *I don't understand why some people have plenty*
> *While others just barely get by.*
> *Why do new waves of trouble keep pounding around me?*
> *Before yesterday's waves ebb away?*
> *But in moments like these when my faith starts to falter,*
> *God's Spirit just tenderly whispers to say:*
> *"There's a reason, there's a plan, there's a purpose and there's a goal,*
> *And Jesus, who loves us more than anyone can,*
> *Is still very much in control."*[6]

Again, a key to surviving these events and growing through them is to surround ourselves with trusted, godly friends and counselors. That means developing friendships with people we know will stand with us, speak truth to us, and point us to God's sovereignty and love in any and all situations. Who can you call at 3:00 a.m. when the roof of your life falls in? We all need someone who will come when we call, someone who loves us and cares enough to be inconvenienced and pressured by our needs. It's not a call we make lightly, but we know our friend will be there.

In addition, keep trusting God. He has your best interests at heart, and His perfect plan for you will be finalized. These are not trite words; they are foundational biblical truth, given to the nation of Israel after the prophet Jeremiah predicted that the nation would spend years in captivity and slavery, suffering in Babylon. Jeremiah went on to say that God wasn't finished with His people: "'I know the plans I have for you,' declares the LORD, 'plans to prosper you and not to harm you, plans to give you hope and a future.'"[7] God had a plan for His people, despite their years of suffering. He has plans for us as well, no matter what difficulties we face. Life isn't finished until God determines it is.

Every life is valuable. Every life is significant. And as long as you have breath, your life is not over; God has something more for you. Begin now to see the purpose God has for you.

QUESTIONS FOR REFLECTION

1. What is the best way to face traumatic events in life?
2. How can we accept the death of infants and young people?
3. What does God want us to learn through difficult times?
4. Discuss whether or not there are "unfinished" lives.

HEADACHE
TROUBLE
PAIN
BANKRUPTCY
LOSS
DEBT
HORROR
WORRIES
STRESS

CHAPTER 9

UNFINISHED SUFFERING

In this one book are the two most interesting personalities in the whole world—God and you. The Bible is the story of God and man, a love story in which you and I must write our own ending, our unfinished autobiography of the creature and the Creator.

FULTON OURSLER

When one of our granddaughters was two years old, she was hospitalized with a severe respiratory infection. The children's rooms in the hospital were pleasant, the walls covered with teddy bears and frolicking baby animals. Televisions played children's videos, and parents were provided beds to stay with the kids twenty-four hours a day. The child's primary room was pleasant most of the time, but if a painful procedure was needed, the child was taken down the hall to the "hurt room."

Doesn't that sound a lot like life? We are doing fine, and then suddenly something happens and we find ourselves in a hurting place.

No one escapes suffering in this life. No one. Jesus affirmed this when He said, "I have told you all this so that you will have peace of heart and mind. Here on earth you will have many trials and sorrows; but cheer up, for I have overcome the world."[1]

Some people encounter suffering early in life, like the granddaughter of our dear friends who was three years old when she was diagnosed with leukemia. As we write, she is undergoing strenuous treatment. The prognosis is hopeful, but she has suffered much.

Others encounter suffering as teens and young adults, perhaps when their friends betray them, their hopes are disappointed, or their parents get divorced. Jerry was only a baby when his parents divorced, and he lived with his mother and grandfather until he was eight. Initially, the divorce had little impact on him, as his grandfather stepped into the role of father in Jerry's life. They lived in a small town, and Jerry was happy, carefree, and unconcerned with any problems his mother might have had.

But when he was eight and a half, his mother remarried and they moved from that tiny town to the city of Spokane, Washington. Jerry was taken from his grandfather, removed from all that was familiar except his mother, and introduced to a new stepfather. It was a painful, traumatic time, and he was allowed no voice in the dramatic changes in his life. He was grieving the loss of his grandfather, and he had to adjust to a new environment, new family, and new friends. He was frightened, sad, and apprehensive of the future. But good came out of his suffering in that it prepared him to hear the good news of Jesus.

Even though God brings good out of suffering, it always leaves scars and memories. It is never finished. The hurt decreases with time, but the tenderness is still there. Infidelity in a marriage can be forgiven and repaired, but the hurt remains. Words spoken reside in a memory bank that never gets erased. Like Jacob in the Old Testament, we walk with a limp the rest of our lives.

Suffering comes primarily in two forms: physical and emotional, with many subcategories falling under each one and typically producing unfinished issues in our lives.

PHYSICAL SUFFERING

Mary, who is of northern European (specifically Norwegian and Swedish) descent, has red hair and freckled skin prone to sunburn easily. As a child, she hated those freckles and her long, braided red hair. She once rubbed her skin raw trying to scrub her freckles away using her mother's harsh sink cleanser. Later, during her college days, she made a remark to her roommate about her dislike of freckles. The roommate responded, "Just be glad they're not pimples!" Good perspective.

When Mary accepted that she was made as God decided she should be made, she could forget her freckles and focus on the important things of life. (And who knows, maybe her natural coloring could be traced back to that rogue explorer Erik the Red!) This experience provided her with a foundation for accepting herself as right and complete in God's eyes.

God's plan is perfect. He knows our human bodies. He knew us before we were conceived. In fact, He knew us before He created the world and had a place to put us. He knew every detail of our bodies long before any sonogram picked out the details. Confidence in His goodness brings peace and contentment in the midst of imperfect bodies and complex illnesses.

This confidence is essential for those whose physical suffering lasts for a lifetime. In our culture of modern medical miracles, we are led to expect healing and help for all problems. But that isn't always the case. Some physical limitations persist unchecked and unrelenting in spite of prayer and medical help. But when we accept them, trusting in God's goodness, we find peace and purpose in our suffering.

That was the case with Bud, a dear friend who suffered from cerebral palsy. His distorted speech and twisted limbs created physical and social troubles that followed him throughout his life. But he was a hero. He struggled to surmount his limitations, improving his speech by singing hymns and through speech therapy exercises. He learned to play tennis, and he purchased and operated a printing business, which required an exacting use of his misshapen fingers. Even though his restrictions afflicted him for his entire life, Bud never complained about his difficulties. He remained a friend and counselor until his death.

Some physical problems appear early in life and have a lingering effect. Chronic problems and pain can result from a battleground injury, devastating car accident, or debilitating illness later in life. Sometimes a person has a weak physical constitution for unknown reasons. This was the case with Mary's mother.

We do not lose heart. Though outwardly we are wasting away, yet inwardly we are being renewed day by day. — 2 Corinthians 4:16

Mother endured a slow, progressive, and rare neurological disorder for twelve years before it finally claimed her life. She was a musically gifted, active, vibrant woman. She was raising five children and supporting her husband in ministry when the disease struck her. It finally took a trip to the famed Mayo Clinic in Rochester, Minnesota, to diagnose the unusual illness. She gradually lost fine, then gross, motor control, and eventually was confined to bed, yet her inner spirit and confidence in God seemed to grow proportionately stronger.

By her final days, the two of us were married and living across the continent from Mary's parents. One day her father wrote to tell us what her mother had said that day. He had been working away from the home for the day, and when he returned she said in surprise, "Are you home already? The days pass so quickly. There are so many people to pray for." She accepted her limitations as God's perfect will for her life and found peace and purpose in her sickness.

We are all God's creatures. He has formed us as He wishes:

You created my inmost being;
you knit me together in my mother's womb.
I praise you because I am fearfully and wonderfully made;

your works are wonderful,
I know that full well.
My frame was not hidden from you
*   when I was made in the secret place.*
When I was woven together in the depths of the earth,
*   your eyes saw my unformed body.*[2]

EMOTIONAL SUFFERING

Emotional suffering can, for a time, be hidden and invisible to others. The inner hurt goes deep and can be incredibly hard to search out and heal. This process may take days, months, or even years to complete.

All of us have suffered or will suffer emotional damage during our lifetimes. What brings about this deep emotional hurt? It comes from many negative experiences, including harsh words from those who love us, taunting by classmates, unjust accusations, rejection, failure, loss, and abandonment.

Clara worked in a day-care center for nearly ten years. She loved the children and was always surrounded by laughing, happy toddlers. Nap time was the only occasion when she didn't hear, "Miss Clara, Miss Clara, look at me." "Miss Clara, see what I did." "Miss Clara, I love you."

When a new employee was hired, the administration asked Clara to train her. For some reason never determined, the new employee took an immediate dislike to Clara, resisted her advice, and ignored her instructions. After two weeks, the new employee went to the administration and accused Clara of sexually molesting two little boys. Although there was no evidence and certainly no history of such behavior, the administration reluctantly put Clara on leave. By law, a report had to be made to the authorities, and Clara was summoned to the police station for an interview. After a long and painful time of research and investigation, Clara was cleared of any charges. The other employee was dismissed and Clara was rehired.

But the emotional scars remained. Clara continued to treat the children with care and love, but the exuberance was missing. She often was seen with silent tears flowing, and it troubled the children. After five more years, Clara gave up the job she loved and took a computer job in a small office. She never completely lost the sick, heartbroken feeling that stemmed from the cruel and false accusations.

Clara's emotional trauma and the resulting unfinished healing give us an extreme example of the emotional suffering some people endure. Not all emotional blows are as difficult as Clara's. And no one can feel the depth of emotional pain, except the person experiencing it. Whether an emotional hurt comes from a minor insult, false accusation, or major rejection, the resulting pain can last a lifetime. Healing comes with time, prayer, the love of trusted friends, and sometimes the help of professional counseling.

Only the person involved can know his own bitterness or joy—no one else can really share it. —Proverbs 14:10 (TLB)

Some emotional issues remain unresolved and unfinished. With God's help, we can learn to live with a new reality, forging a new life and new relationships as we remember that final resolution comes from God at work in our hearts and in the hearts of people around us. We can take steps to find joy in what we *do* have rather than focusing on what we *don't* have. God's comfort and strength in our suffering brings healing and peace and, yes, even joy.

Dear brothers and sisters, when troubles come your way, consider it an opportunity for great joy. For you know that when your faith is tested, your endurance has a chance to grow. So let it grow, for when your endurance is fully developed, you will be perfect and complete, needing nothing.[3]

This is a wonderful promise! Suffering of any kind isn't wasted; God has a use for every pain we feel.

SECURE IN GOD'S FINISHING SCHOOL

Everyone has hidden suffering—even Christians. Our belief in Jesus does not exempt us from suffering. We live in a fallen world and will experience the effects of the sin and trouble that inundate our world. The simple request "Tell me your story" opens a series of memories, both good and bad. At the first telling, there are the successes and joys, but soon, even with strangers, small stories of trials and disappointments emerge. A trembling voice or tears reveal the depth of the pain.

When our son was murdered, the emotional pain and grief was so strong that it hurt to breathe. Eating became a necessary ordeal and our stomachs hurt day and night. Restful sleep was impossible. We learned the meaning of a broken heart. The horror of losing our son in such a brutal way meant we couldn't think well, we couldn't make decisions, we lived in a mental fog, and tears flowed endlessly. At some point, we began to turn gradually from thinking about our loss and the years we would never have with Steve to remembering his life and living with gratitude that we'd had him with us for thirty years. The sharp pangs of early grief began to slowly diminish.

It takes a long time to recover from a deep emotional hurt, and in some ways, we never do. Psalm 119:50 assures us of God's presence and help through all our difficulties: "My comfort in my suffering is this: Your promise preserves my life."

Suffering builds us into a person of beauty and character that only God can make. We become the recipients of grace and love from God and others and experience the healing that can come from Him alone. We walk out of that dark tunnel into His light and freedom as we hear Him whisper, "I am with you."[4] "I will sustain you."[5] "Well done, good and faithful servant!"[6]

Yes, our suffering remains unfinished; our lives are still unfinished. But we are secure in God's finishing school. As the Master Potter, He is remaking us into a new creation, drawing us close to Himself and molding us into the image of Christ.

QUESTIONS FOR REFLECTION

1. What part does suffering play in our lives?
2. If suffering is inescapable and rarely finished, what are appropriate actions and attitudes toward it and toward God?
3. What parts of suffering do get finished? What parts finish and still affect us? What parts are never finished?
4. What are you learning from your suffering now?

PART 2

FINISHING WELL, WITHOUT REGRETS

Mexico 1968

Out of the cold darkness he came. John Stephen Akhwari of Tanzania entered at the far end of the stadium, pain hobbling his every step, his leg bloody and bandaged. The winner of the marathon had been declared over an hour earlier. Only a few spectators remained, but the lone runner pressed on.

As he crossed the finish line, the small crowd roared out with appreciation. Afterward, a reporter asked the runner why he had not stopped running the race since he had no chance of winning. He seemed confused by the question. Finally, he answered, "My country did not send me to Mexico City to start the race. They sent me to finish."[1]

CHAPTER 10

GETTING A SECOND WIND

*This I am resolved on; to run where I can, to go when
I cannot run, and to creep when I cannot go. . . . My mind
is beyond the river that hath no bridge, though I am, as you
see, but of a feeble mind. . . . Sometimes the greatest
inspiration for living is when your mind is beyond that
river that hath no bridge. Were it not for that assurance,
many experiences of life would be unbearable.*

MR. FEEBLE MIND[2]

One of the saddest epitaphs ever written was for Jehoram, King of
Judah. "He passed away, to no one's regret."[3] No one cared that
this king had died. His life was a disgrace.

None of us wants such words to be said of us. We want our lives to
have meaning, purpose, and impact. The good news is that, regardless
of our past failures, this goal is within our reach. We can all finish well
and leave a godly legacy.

But finishing well in our physical, emotional, and spiritual lives is a
challenge. It requires new energy, purpose, and stamina to keep going.
It requires a second wind. What is this second wind? It is:

• An extra boost of energy, often when it seems there is no energy
left

- Another chance in life, when it seems that a previous life is over
- A time of refocusing to put efforts where they count the most

Many people in second marriages get a second wind: the desire to do it right this time and not repeat past mistakes. So do recovering alcoholics and drug addicts and people who have resolved to overcome an illness or grief.

All of us need a second wind a number of times throughout our lives. It is not just for the last dash to the finish line but rather repeatedly in order for us to keep going. It's a renewed energy that restores every part of life.

Jerry needed a second wind when he retired from his Air Force career and suddenly had no more authority or responsibility. Within days, his assistant asked, "Do you realize that your phone calls have reduced by about 50 percent?" Jerry adjusted to this ending in his life by continuing his involvement as a volunteer in Air Force–related endeavors: the Air Force Association, the Department of Astronautics at the United States Air Force Academy, and local business and military connections. These relationships keep him involved and connected to people.

When his roles as international president of The Navigators and chairman of the U.S. board of directors at The Navigators ended, it caused us to not only reflect on our contribution but also understand that any future involvement would be a matter of influence and counsel, not authority. Now we need a "second wind" in terms of our contributions.

Paul clearly had this second wind in mind when he wrote to his friends in Corinth,

Do you not know that in a race all the runners run, but only one gets the prize? Run in such a way as to get the prize. Everyone who competes in the games goes into strict training. They do it to get a crown that will not last; but we do it to get a crown that

will last forever. Therefore I do not run like a man running aimlessly; I do not fight like a man beating the air. No, I beat my body and make it my slave so that after I have preached to others, I myself will not be disqualified for the prize.[4]

The people of Corinth knew the athletic games of that day, as the biennial Isthmian Games were staged there. These games were second only to the Olympics, and the Corinthians watched these athletes train. They knew the harsh regimen they endured in diet and discipline. In this passage, Paul uses *running* and *runners* as metaphors for Christians running in the race of life. He says to stick to strict training and then reminds us that we are not competing for a crown of olive branches that will wither away in days but rather for one that has eternal significance. His challenge to us is:

- To run with aim and purpose
- To work with focus and direction toward a worthy goal
- To fight the battle of life with directed vigor, not with fitful and empty attacks (not beating the air)
- To exercise physical, mental, and spiritual disciplines to run well and not fall short at the end of life

In the Isthmian games, competitors would be disqualified for breaking the rules during the race and for not using the prescribed training regimens. In the race Paul speaks of, everyone can win and be rewarded.

All of us will face times in life when we need a second wind, a new lease on life. But how do we get it?

ENVISION THE ENDGAME AND DEVELOP A GAME PLAN

In athletics, we often use the term *endgame.* In professional basketball, people believe that the game is determined in the last five minutes. In baseball, the last innings often see the use of a relief pitcher who is credited with the "save."

The endgame in life is equally important. In our younger years, we contemplate the future and the idea of finishing the rearing of our children, finishing our career, finishing the goals we hope to accomplish and the things we want to do. But no matter our age, we need to act with the endgame in mind. This requires envisioning what it looks like to finish well. Take some time right now to ponder what it would mean to finish your life well.

A word of warning: Don't think of yourself in the last hours of your life, in a hospital bed, with death hovering nearby; think of yourself in your fruitful and more mature years, when you still have the possibility to make corrections and adjustments. Identify five to ten statements that identify what needs to happen in your life in order for you to finish well. Go beyond some of the most obvious godly or philosophical responses, such as:

- "I have served God wholeheartedly."
- "My children are following God and doing well."
- "I have served my fellow man."
- "I have loved my spouse and children and done all I could to serve them."

We want you to broaden your thinking to include areas on which you spend most of your time and energy. What would it look like for you to finish well in the following areas?

- Career and work
- Finances
- Parenting and children
- Marriage
- Spiritual life

This list is not in order of importance but indicates the areas of most concern and worry. At the end of life, few people say, "I wish I had spent more time at the office." While true, most of us put significant amounts of time into our work for a number of reasons, including job security, the inherent pressure of our work, and because we find satisfaction and significance in our jobs. How can you approach your work, marriage, finances, and so on with the endgame in mind? That is what we want you to focus on.

Take some time now to do the following exercise:

At the end of my life, I will be satisfied if . . .

1. _____.

2. _____.

3. _____.

4. _____.

5. _____.

6. _____.

7. _____.

8. _____.

9. _____.

10. _____.

Now that you have identified what needs to be true of your life in order for you to finish well, you need a game plan to be sure you get there.

As an avid older handball player, Jerry has experienced numerous muscle injuries. He used to tough it out, trying his best to recover with no external help. On one occasion, he tripped, rolled, and slammed his back and shoulder into the wall. Fearing that the shoulder was broken, he went to his family physician, who prescribed physical therapy. The physical therapist laid out a careful plan of recovery, including treatments and exercises of several types.

What the physical therapist did with Jerry was similar to the game plans a coach lays out for his team. Although the game plan always gets modified during the game, there is always a plan. The coach doesn't just say, "Okay, team, go play your best." The team watches game films, learns the strengths and weaknesses of the opponents, and practices with the game plan in mind.

Similarly, we need a game plan that outlines our plans and preparations for finishing well in the physical, spiritual, occupational, familial, and emotional areas of life.

The physical has to do with maintaining our health: daily exercise, a healthy diet, and regular medical assessments.

The spiritual plan focuses on our spiritual growth. It includes involvement in reaching out to others, regular times of Scripture reading and prayer, developing our knowledge of the Bible through teaching and study, and learning to apply it to specific areas of life.

A game plan for our work takes into account our gifts, experience, education, and needs.

We also need a game plan for how to develop our marriage relationships and relationships with family members. We often neglect these relationships until a crisis emerges. Singleness (by choice), divorce, and loss of a spouse are special circumstances that alter our game plans.

Each of these game plans brings emotional issues into our lives that cannot be discounted or neglected. The pressures from health issues, work, and family affect us emotionally in ways that are not immediately obvious. Over time, they can lead to discouragement and depression. Therefore, we need to protect and develop our emotional health with the same attention we give our physical well-being.

All of these areas have been addressed to some degree in earlier chapters. Our point here is to encourage you to develop a realistic game plan. We have found that simple yearly goals help us focus.

SEE YOURSELF AS A VALUED CHILD OF GOD

How you think about yourself affects your life and actions in profound ways, including your ability to get a second wind in the second half of life. Have you heard these provocative statements?

- You are what you do.
- You are what you think.
- You are what you eat.
- You are whom you associate with.

Are those statements true? What deeper issues do they highlight? We often consider the perception others have of us, but the more important issue is how we see ourselves.

Our identities control so much of what we do and think. Teenagers worry about being in the right group. Men want to drive the right car. Women want to have the right clothes. Some peoples' identities cause them to demand the limelight. A friend of ours was on an airline flight in which a middle-aged man walked up and down the aisle asking people, "Do you know who I am?" He had been a professional football player and wanted everyone to know it. He had a warped identity.

Where does our identity come from? Typically, it comes from either our external person or our internal person.

The external person. This is the person others see.

For men it is often defined by:

- Work—what we do: bricklayer, carpenter, computer analyst, lawyer, doctor, engineer, salesperson, farmer, laborer
- Success—promotions, salary, title, accomplishments
- Toys—cars, skis, cabins, workshops
- Athletic ability or hobbies—sports, hunting, fishing, handball

- Gifts and abilities—intellect, leadership, creativity, professional skills
- Education

For women, their external person is often defined by:

- Appearance
- Housing
- Children's accomplishments
- Professional achievements
- Husband's position
- Education

The items listed are not bad or evil. Who doesn't want success, position, and education? Each of these can be good and worthy goals. The problem emerges when we look to these things for our true identity. Placing our trust or identity in these areas leads to disappointment as difficulties invade our lives. If we lose our job, miss a promotion, become ill, go bankrupt, lose a house, develop facial wrinkles, or parent rebellious children, our identity begins to crumble. If we buy into the myth that external things define us, we will be devastated. If we understand that they are temporary, fragile, and external, we can move to a truer identity.

If we do not understand the fragile nature of external identity, we:

- Lose confidence
- Lose perspective
- Lose marriages
- Lose purpose

But when we base our identity on the internal person, we:

- Gain confidence
- Gain perspective

- Keep our marriages
- Gain purpose
- Gain a second wind

The internal person. This is your true self—the person God sees. A biblical man or woman is one who knows God's purposes. The trite saying "God didn't make no junk" is true. He created us with care and love. We are loved with an everlasting love and have eternal value with Him and for Him. The task is to see ourselves as valued sons and daughters of God, made in His image and redeemed by Jesus.

This can be a challenge, however, because the internal person, though made in God's image, becomes flawed and corrupted by sin. We sin and are prone to sin. We develop habits and character traits that are ungodly. But we can and do change. Christ came so that we could overcome the power of sin in our lives. The message of the gospel is the message of transformation. We are daily being transformed into God's image.[5] It is a process, not an event.

Finishing well and getting a second wind require envisioning the endgame, developing a game plan, and living up to the person we are in Christ. Regardless of mistakes we have made, God, through the power of the Holy Spirit, can rebuild, purify, and change us.

QUESTIONS FOR REFLECTION

1. What makes it so easy or tempting to give up?
2. Describe what a game plan would look like for you.
3. How would you describe your "internal" man or woman?
4. Where do you need a second wind now?

CHAPTER 11

DEFUSING TIME BOMBS

*Life is what happens to you while you're busy making
other plans.*

JOHN LENNON

Most of us, whether we admit it or not, are control freaks. We want to make our own decisions. We resist being told what to do. We value our independence and want to decide how to live our lives and create our destinies.

There are many aspects of our lives over which we have a measure of control:

- **Our spiritual lives.** We make decisions regarding our spiritual disciplines and growth. We decide if we will spend time in the Scriptures daily. We decide if we will obey what we know.
- **Our emotional lives.** Emotions are complex. One area we can control is our attitudes — toward people, God, and circumstances.
- **Our physical lives.** Although illness and genetics will ultimately impact us, we can do much to enhance our physical well-being.
- **Our relationships.** We can decide to foster and develop good relationships and deep friendships. In conflict situations, we can choose to become peacemakers.

- **Family issues.** Our children, parents, and extended family
  provide us with joy and sorrow, yet most families experience
  some level of tension and conflict. We can determine our
  involvement in these disagreements.

Even so, there is much in life that we can't control. It is important
to know the difference. Understanding our limits on what we can and
cannot control frees us to work with reality and defuse issues and
attitudes sown over time that will harm us if unaddressed. We call these
time bombs.

Years ago, Jerry was traveling in a disputed and war-torn central
European area on a road that was a minefield. Some of the mines had
been removed and defused; others could be detonated when someone
stepped on them or drove over them. To avoid that danger, the soldiers
had to closely follow the designated route. Similarly, in life there are
time bombs that, if not defused, will explode, preventing us from living
up to our spiritual heritage and destiny.

Such is the situation with many aspects of our personal lives.
Time bombs swirl in and around us, acting like acid that slowly eats
the material it touches. Though we may not see fully their effects at
the moment, left unattended these sins spoil our relationships with
God and others, thus diminishing our ability to finish well and live
without regrets.

In this chapter, we want to explore some of these time bombs. They
are not listed in any order of priority nor discussed in great depth. We
want to bring them to your attention and allow the Holy Spirit to speak
to you.

UNRESOLVED RELATIONAL ISSUES

Conflict is unavoidable, a part of human life. Offenses that lead to
breaks in friendship occur almost daily. We see acidic and brutal accusations in political discussions and strategies as well as among friends and

coworkers. Churches split over theological disagreements or conflicts over decisions. Parents, siblings, and other relatives experience conflict that remains unresolved in their lifetimes. The result is sadness, loss, loneliness, and destructive consequences passed on to future generations.

> If it is possible, as far as it depends on you, live at peace with everyone. —Romans 12:18

Scripture tells us to do all we can to resolve conflict on the basis of love. The parable of the unmerciful servant in Matthew 18:23-35 teaches us that if we don't forgive those with whom we have a conflict, God will not forgive us. Several proverbs warn of the consequences of unresolved conflict in broken relationships: "An offended brother is more unyielding than a fortified city, and disputes are like the barred gates of a citadel."[1] It also warns that the Lord hates "a man who stirs up dissension among brothers."[2]

Broken relationships destroy families, churches, and organizations. Left unresolved, relational conflicts will demolish our spiritual fiber and lead us to the next time bomb.

BITTERNESS AND ANGER

The author of Hebrews instructed, "See to it that no one comes short of the grace of God; that no root of bitterness springing up causes trouble, and by it many be defiled."[3] Unresolved conflict degenerates into bitterness and anger. These emotions not only defile and destroy *us*, they also wound and infect others. Synonyms of *bitterness*—*resentment*, *animosity*, and *hostility*—give us further insight into its destructive nature. These attitudes injure our emotional lives and our physical health.

Anger shows in a person's speech, attitude, and even physical appearance. At some time or another, you've probably met someone and thought, *That is an angry person.* Anger destroys friendships and marriages and creates dissension. "Angry people stir up a lot of discord; the intemperate stir up trouble."[4] It frightens children, who are not emotionally equipped to handle an adult's anger. It cripples our ability to work with others. It is self-destructive and eats at us physically and emotionally, leaving in its wake ulcers and sleepless nights. No wonder Proverbs says, "A wise man restrains his anger and overlooks insults. This is to his credit."[5]

How can you defuse this time bomb? Simply guard your tongue and be patient: "Everyone should be quick to listen, slow to speak and slow to become angry."[6]

JEALOUSY AND ENVY

Envy and jealousy develop when we are dissatisfied with ourselves or what we possess, which is why Scripture offers these warnings about these time bombs:

I observed all the work and ambition motivated by envy. What a waste! Smoke. And spitting into the wind.[7]

Clean house! Make a clean sweep of malice and pretense, envy and hurtful talk.[8]

Where jealousy and selfish ambition exist, there is disorder and every evil thing.[9]

These are strong words provoking strong emotions. Jealousy and envy ultimately wreak their havoc in our lives. We defuse these time bombs by being content with who we are and what we have and by rejoicing in others' successes and joys.[10]

DISCORD AND DISSENSION

These sins are on the devastating list of acts of the sinful nature in Galatians 5:19-21. We see them all around us—disunity, conflict, arguments, and disagreements. According to this passage, these sins rank with the sins of idolatry and sexual immorality.

Proverbs makes a connection between anger and dissension:

A hot-tempered man stirs up dissension, but a patient man calms a quarrel.[11]

An angry man stirs up dissension, and a hot-tempered one commits many sins.[12]

This deadly combination breaks friendships, destroys churches, and devastates families. If you frequently engage in conflict and discord, look first at your own heart before blaming others. The antidote is to guard your thoughts and tongue.

While disagreement is not wrong, underlying anger and hostility that lead to discord are sin. The counterattack to these destructive time bombs is to "keep in step with the Spirit. Let us not become conceited, provoking and envying each other."[13]

GOSSIP

Proverbs warns,

Don't talk about your neighbors behind their backs—no slander or gossip, please.[14]

Mean people spread mean gossip; their words smart and burn.[15]

Gossip is saying something that may or may not be true but doesn't need to be said. It spreads some bit of information that sullies another's reputation or character. It destroys friendships and undermines trust. Gossip offers "news" or "information for prayer," putting another person in a bad light.

Here are some phrases that qualify as gossip:

- "Jack just got royally chewed out by his boss."
- "Marilyn is pregnant again. Can you believe it?"
- "That car must have cost a fortune."
- "Joe and Ann are really struggling in their marriage. We need to pray for them."
- "There is really a lot more to that story than they told you."

Why do we gossip? Sometimes to give an impression that we are in the know or to build our own egos. Sadly, sometimes it is a deliberate statement meant to hurt another person or his or her reputation.

Gossip can become a pattern of speech that is hard to correct. To defuse this time bomb, learn to guard your lips and let others tell their own news, good or bad.

FAILURE TO GROW AND CHANGE

Each of us tends to freeze in our past in some way. Whether it is clothing style, hairdo, or attitude, we stay the same rather than change. Consequently, we stop growing and developing, which is the first sign of decay and death. The failure to grow is not a matter of age but of attitude and action.[16]

A telltale indication of this time bomb is criticism of the present, as evidenced by comments such as, "Can you believe these young people? Why can't they just do it the way we always have?"

To defuse this time bomb, we need to be open to new ideas and new ways of thinking. We need to make adjustments to the world as we find it today.

HAVING LITTLE OR NO PURPOSE

The lack of purpose is a time bomb that leads to lethargy and laziness. Purpose keeps us motivated; a lack of purpose kills.

Statistics indicate that people, especially men, who retire at age fifty-five die sooner than those who retire at sixty-five or older. Women live longer in general. Women working in the home may live longer because their purpose does not change with a husband's retirement.[17] However, as women participate more in the workplace, their death rates are rising to match those of men.

Of course, statistics do not determine our life spans; God does. However, that doesn't mean we should ignore the implication of these facts. Many people derive a sense of purpose from their jobs, and it is important that they adjust their sense of purpose upon retirement.

One of Jerry's mentors was J. Oswald Sanders, who was a lawyer and the director of China Inland Mission (now OMF). After "retirement," he was constantly in demand as a speaker, and he continued writing. Shortly before his death from cancer at age ninety, he told Jerry, "Well, I am writing my last book. I have thought that several books ago was my last, but this really is." His indomitable spirit, wise counsel, and positive attitude were contagious.

If we want to finish well, we need a purpose for living. We need something that occupies our mind and time. When people cannot find a job, they become despondent and depressed. They lose hope and purpose. We need something that makes us get out of bed in the morning.

The Bible speaks often about purpose. We know that God has an ultimate purpose for us (we are "called according to his purpose"[18]). Paul clearly understood God's purpose for him.

For this purpose I was appointed a herald and an apostle — I am telling the truth, I am not lying — and a teacher of the true faith to the Gentiles.[19]

You, however, know all about my teaching, my way of life, my purpose, faith, patience, love, endurance.[20]

Followers of Christ have a central purpose to glorify and serve God and grow in Christlikeness.

Proverbs says, "The purposes of a man's heart are deep waters, but a man of understanding draws them out."[21] This tells us that our purpose comes from deep within us. It is an inner motivation. "Form your purpose by asking for counsel, then carry it out using all the help you can get."[22]

When you know your purpose, it deepens your motivation to keep going and finish well. It gives you that second wind.

SEARCH FOR TIME BOMBS

Life is a long-distance race. We inevitably get tired and wonder if we can keep going. The time bombs we have discussed, when not defused, can cause us to give up, so take time to reflect on the following questions and search for time bombs that might be in your life. Ask the Holy Spirit to show you which of these times bombs you need to defuse and to give the strength and resolve to keep going and finish well. Then act on what He shows you!

QUESTIONS FOR REFLECTION

1. What can you personally control, and what can you not control?
2. Which time bombs are most relevant to you?
3. What can you do to defuse those time bombs?
4. What are the big issues for you in finishing well?

CHAPTER 12

BUILDING AND REBUILDING

Many people dream of success. To me, success can be achieved only through repeated failure and introspection. In fact, success represents the 1 percent of your work that results from 99 percent that is called failure.

SOICHIRO HONDA

We live at the base of the Rocky Mountains in Colorado. In October, the aspen trees change color from green to brilliant yellow. Spectators by the thousands flock to the mountains to see this incredibly colorful display. The same autumn kaleidoscope of colors infuses the states of New England with a marvelous panoply of colors that no photograph can fully capture. With the first frost or strong wind, the leaves fall. This is natural decay. Then in the spring, new growth begins the process all over.

The human body goes through a comparable process. At least two major organs decay and rebuild, not annually but almost three times a year: our skin and our muscles. We can do little about the skin except to protect it from radiation and abuse, but the muscle system is different. We need to exercise our muscles or they will atrophy.

This is even true for young people. One of our grandsons recently broke three bones in his foot and had to wear a cast and brace for several weeks. Within two weeks, his affected leg had atrophied in the calf area by almost half. Because he's young, the normal activities of youth will do the necessary rebuilding. However, as we age, our muscle systems do not rebuild without focused effort. If older people do not exercise, the leg and lower body muscles get weak and do not rebuild. This causes them to totter, stumble, and fall.

Similar to our muscle systems, our personal lives need regular, determined, and focused building and rebuilding. We've talked in other chapters about the imperative of building ourselves spiritually, physically, and emotionally and of building and rebuilding our marriages, careers, and parenting. Sadly, we often wait to build and rebuild until a crisis strikes. Then life breaks. What we've built starts to crumble and we are forced to give up or rebuild.

Understand that we are not talking about New Year's resolutions, those wish lists that make you feel good for about three weeks until they get put aside or forgotten. We are talking about a determined resolution that changes the way we live.

The longer we wait to rebuild parts of our lives, the harder it becomes. But it's never too late to start. At age seventy, Jerry decided to learn how to play the cello. He has always loved music, and for years he performed vocally in several contexts. Then he developed a polyp on his vocal chords from the stress after our son's death. More vocal chord issues emerged until Jerry could no longer sing.

So he found a teacher and began learning to play the cello. Last summer he even went to a music camp and was in the beginning orchestra with twelve- to fourteen-year-olds! He really worked hard but still couldn't master some fast scales. He simply had not practiced enough for the muscle memory in his fingers to keep up. Age and ability might have something to do with it! Building a new skill takes hard work, focus, time, and determination. Nothing just happens. If we don't rebuild, we stagnate.

Let's take a closer look at some of the areas we need to build and rebuild.

AREAS FOR BUILDING OR REBUILDING

Building and rebuilding require careful thinking, planning, and time. You cannot do everything at once. Be patient. Think in the time frame of the next two years. This is a reasonable and realistic period of time to effectively address a number of important issues.

Only a few things are urgent. You will know which areas to work on immediately. (You may want to review a few of the earlier chapters to refresh your thinking on the issues that the Spirit of God has already brought to your attention.)

Your family. We have not met anyone (including ourselves) who has a perfect marriage or perfect children. When we are unhappy in our marriage relationship, we are unhappy in life. Strained marriages create tense and miserable children who are emotionally harmed. So if your marriage is struggling, don't delay the rebuilding in this area. Seek help aggressively.

Your family will be with you for your entire life. No matter what your past family relationships have been like, you can now begin to repair and rebuild or keep building on the foundation you have already laid. (Review chapter 4 for help in rebuilding your family.)

Your work/career. Stan was a young military officer who was passed over for promotion three times. From a human perspective, his career was over, yet he decided to focus on rebuilding areas he had neglected in his work. To everyone's surprise, he was eventually promoted to full colonel. Stan saw what needed correcting in his work life and set about working hard to overcome his past. He saw the fruit of his efforts as he changed his attitude and actions. As a follower of Christ, he also realized that his past performance was not a good testimony. With God's help, he overcame nearly impossible odds to continue his career.

What aspects of your work or career might you focus on to build or rebuild? Ask God to show you what you can do to strengthen this part of your life. In uncertain economic times, work is never assured. For many people, a career is less important than simply having a job that supports the family. Rearing and caring for children and keeping up a home is equally important work. (Review chapter 5 for help in rebuilding your work and career.)

Your spiritual life. Is there one aspect of life that is *not* spiritual? No. It is all spiritual. The trap of religiosity and "spiritual" activities undermines the reality and significance of the totality of life.

Hank was a leader as an Air Force Academy cadet among his fellow believers, but early in his career, he battled some sin issues and became so discouraged that he walked away from God. Eighteen years later, after we made many attempts to contact him, he wrote in a Christmas card that he had returned to following Christ. His wife was not a believer; his children were rebellious and in trouble with the law. It took Stan years to rebuild his walk with God, but he did. Today he has a vibrant testimony for Christ, and his wife is also a believer. It is never too late to rebuild.

As Hank's story shows, your initial spiritual birth and your ongoing growth are vital. Keep in mind that you can't rebuild something that has never been built. So the first task is to assure the reality of your personal relationship to God in Christ. What is your current status with God? What points of commitment have you made throughout your life? Is the Spirit of God urging you to a deeper and more significant life in Christ? How does your commitment to Christ impact the way you think and live? As you pray over these questions, the Holy Spirit will guide and direct you about how you can either build or rebuild your spiritual life. (Review chapter 7 for help in rebuilding your spiritual life.)

Your physical and emotional lives. We owe it to ourselves and our families to be better stewards of our bodies. The discipline we need to work on weight, exercise, and diet is obvious. No amount of cajoling on our part will help you change. We urge simple, attainable goals. Develop accountability with a trusted friend or an organization. Plan on slow, progressive change.

The emotional life is more complex. Many things can sabotage our emotional well-being: relationships, illnesses, drugs, children's problems, and family issues. If you struggle with any of these, don't keep it to yourself; talk with a counselor, pastor, or friend.

This is easier said than done, of course. Acknowledging emotional needs is one of the most difficult things we can do. When we speak at conferences, one question we often ask is "Have you ever been seriously depressed?" Many people raise their hands. Then we ask, "How many of you told someone else that you were depressed?" Very few men raise their hands, while most of the women say they have talked with at least one friend. Men often find it more difficult to ask for emotional help than women do.

In recent years, there has been a growing recognition of post-traumatic stress disorder (PTSD) for soldiers who have returned from war deployments. Many seek help. PTSD is also recognized in the lives of those who have suffered severe trauma in other ways. It is never a weakness to admit the need for help. Leaving emotional needs unattended leads to unhappiness, deeper depression, and despair.

Friendships and covenant relationships. Everyone wants and has friends, but not all friends are loyal and deeply committed. Not all friends will speak the truth in love, defend you, and encourage you. That is friendship of the deepest kind. Friendships like this do not develop quickly. They must stand the test of time and trials. They must endure differences, distance, and disagreements. The basis goes beyond fun and enjoyment. Such friendships are not tainted by jealousy or exclusiveness.

We have enjoyed this kind of friendship, and it has been a key element for us in building and rebuilding. For more than twenty-five years, we have had a "covenant" friendship with three other couples. They have intersected and intervened in every aspect of our lives: family, work, walk with God, and more. These friendships go deep because we decided to covenant together for a lifetime. Simply stated, our goal is to help each other walk with Christ the rest of our lives and be accountable to one another. We choose to open our lives and personal affairs to these couples. They do not push their way in. Yet if they see us wandering or sinning, they would speak and intervene.

The eight of us meet twice a year for several days but connect at other times, too. We do not live geographically close, so that adds a complication. In our mobile society, this is not unusual. It means we must work at keeping the relationships fresh and active. All of us have other close friendships that encourage us and hold us accountable.

A friend loves at all times, and a brother is born for adversity. —Proverbs 17:17

Friends of this depth are rare. In an earlier study we did on friendship, we estimated that people experience only three to five deep friendships in a lifetime. Ask God to give you relationships with depth. They will bless your life.

Before we can build and rebuild our lives, we must first recognize the need. Then come focus, energy, and effort. Don't expect quick fixes to overcome a lifetime of poor habits and attitudes, and don't try to do it all at once. Identify specific areas of life and work on them one at a time. Remember, these are not New Year's resolutions but rather life resolutions that are vital to your future.

Friends come and friends go, but a true friend sticks by you like family. —Proverbs 18:24 (MSG)

QUESTIONS FOR REFLECTION

1. Identify two or three areas of your life that need repair, rebuilding, or building.
2. What are the primary barriers you face in rebuilding? In building?
3. Of the five areas we've mentioned, for which do you feel the greatest need?
4. What indications have you had in the last five years that push you to a time of rebuilding?

CHAPTER 13

THE PRESSURE OF UNMET EXPECTATIONS

I am not in this world to live up to other people's expectations, nor do I feel that the world must live up to mine.

FRITZ PERLS

Expectations permeate every facet of our lives. They are present always. Sometimes they energize us to meet our goals. Other times they harm us, pushing us beyond our physical and emotional limits and causing us to say such things as, "Sorry, Dad, I just can't live up to your expectations" and "My husband's expectations of me are impossible to meet. I am not Superwoman!"

Can you relate? Have you ever felt something similar?

Many of us spend our lives trying to live up to the expectations that society, family, and friends place on us. From our earliest years, we experience a set of expectations: to be proficient in sports, get good grades, wear the right clothes, be pretty, be thin, be the best, have sex, not have sex. We try to meet these expectations, and if we don't, it causes feelings of guilt, unworthiness, and frustration. Psychiatrists work daily to free people from the oppressive demands that damage egos and drive people to addictions.

Our purpose here is not to psychoanalyze expectations or even to evaluate their legitimacy. We simply want to help you face and deal with your unmet expectations. We encourage you to evaluate these expectations in the reality of your own life, deciding the extent to which they should influence or control you. We need to free ourselves from many expectations. Others we can and should meet and finish.

Even when we cannot always determine the exact source of the expectation, we can place expectations into distinct categories. They come from self, parents, spouses, children, society, peers, and professions.

UNMET EXPECTATIONS FROM OURSELVES

Most of us go through life feeling we have not measured up to our potential. With that feeling comes a sense of regret or disappointment in ourselves. We have the lingering feeling we could do more, be more.

Jerry had a poignant conversation with a graduate of the Air Force Academy who was dogged by this feeling. The graduate said he was discouraged, battled some chronic illness, had a strained marriage, had difficulties with his children, and was struggling in his faith. When Jerry asked about his work, he was careful to point out that it was low-level, nonexecutive, and not very glamorous. He said, "I have not really lived up to the expectations of an Air Force Academy graduate."

This man saw himself as mediocre. He feared comparison to his fellow graduates, some of whom went on to become generals. He felt weighed down by a bevy of unmet expectations concerning his health, marriage, children, and work. No one had told him that he had not achieved enough. Others see this man as a person of high integrity and honor, but his feelings do not agree.

In order to deal with his own unmet expectations, he had to acknowledge them, evaluate whether they were valid, identify their source, decide what he can change, and then readjust his expectations.

It's not wrong to set a high bar for a big goal. A high jumper who cannot clear a six-foot bar should not quit trying, but he may need to lower the bar. (By the way, the record is seven feet eleven and a half inches indoors and eight feet one-half inch outdoors.) Not everyone is a high-jump champion. So you fall a bit short. The key is to keep going and stay patient. As long as you endeavor to do good and right things in your marriage, relationships, spiritual life, and work, you are "on the way."

Unmet expectations can be your springboard to the future. Start where you are. For example, it may be that before you became a parent, you planned and prepared, believing you would be a loving, patient, ideal mom or dad. When the babies arrived, you were chagrined to discover you could not live up to your ideals. You experienced impatience, anger, and fatigue. Now you relive those moments of poor parenting and feel you have not measured up. The good news is that you can set realistic goals now, such as a goal to apologize to an offended child. Your follow-through on this goal will go a long way to restoring the relationship.

Here are some thoughts on handling your self-imposed expectations:

- Identify them. Name them: your performance as a parent, success as a spouse, or accomplishments in your spiritual life.
- If your expectations have been unmet over a long period of time, evaluate their validity or importance.
- If your unmet expectations are failures that you realistically should have met, then rethinking and readjustment are in order. Write a list of revised expectations that are realistic and desirable.
- Discard expectations that you know do not serve you.

The most onerous of self-imposed expectations relate to what we perceive that God demands of us. We are often performing activities and demands that we think will please Him. Although these activities may be good, they do nothing to create a better standing with God.

You might live with regrets from your past mistakes and sins, but God sees you differently. He sees you as His valued child. He said to Israel, "I have loved you with an everlasting love; I have drawn you with loving-kindness."[1] Your salvation is totally by grace.

The Bible is quite clear on the merits of self- or other-imposed legalism:

You have died with Christ, and he has set you free from the spiritual powers of this world. So why do you keep on following the rules of the world, such as, "Don't handle! Don't taste! Don't touch!"?[2]

A works-driven way of living creates guilt because we can never do enough. As good as our devotional life, Bible studies, and religious activities may be, they do not earn us any favor with God. While we do good works and engage in spiritual activities, we must not deceive ourselves into thinking we are earning God's favor. We are saved by grace, and we walk daily by grace. We are created to do good works but are freed from the obligation to earn any standing with God.[3]

Now let's move to expectations that come from outside ourselves.

UNMET EXPECTATIONS FROM PARENTS

The conflict between parents and their children emerges early in childhood and reaches its zenith during the teen years. Even through adulthood, expectations from parents still ring in our ears. Many moms and dads have the expectation that their children behave well at all times—in the home, at the store, and at family gatherings. They have high expectations regarding their kids' performance in school and sports. They pressure their children to do well and to do better than others, and they reward them for excelling.

If you were raised with these kinds of expectations, you grew up thinking that performance is all that matters. At this point, it is not helpful to judge or blame your parents. You have likely put similar pressure on your own children, with good intentions and poor results. Expectations are the irresistible drive of parents and the inescapable burden of children. In one sense, parental expectations are unavoidable. Certainly, we would not want to have parents who didn't care or expected little of us.

Just realize now as an adult that your parents' unmet expectations of you do not govern how you live. Be who you are before God, releasing your parents' expectations to Him. Give your children the same freedom. Be encouraging, not demanding. Be loving yet realistic and provide the necessary help and training they need. Learn from your own feelings and experiences about how to relate to your children.

Without question, all parents fail in some way. The two of us still, with regret, remember the academic demands we made on our son. He was intellectually gifted, but there were other issues that should have taken precedence over academics. He felt pressure from us that wasn't helpful or necessary. When Steve was attending college, he began struggling with his faith. He communicated that to us and asked, "Will this affect your career with The Navigators?" It was like a knife in our hearts that he would even have to ask. His spiritual life and growth was so much more important to us than our ministry and work.

As our own children grappled with their identities, we realized how little pressure our own parents put on us. They were wonderfully silent and supportive as we made decisions regarding marriage, career, and more.

UNMET EXPECTATIONS FROM ONE'S SPOUSE

Now, this is a road filled with land mines! The one who knows us the best and has our best interests at heart often places the most expectations on us.

We know firsthand just how challenging this can be. Mary is neat; Jerry is messy. Mary is a perfectionist; Jerry is driven. Mary always thinks first of the children; Jerry is always thinking of his job. Mary wants to be listened to; Jerry thinks he is listening. The result is unmet expectations that neither of us is quite able to fulfill.

Marriage is a jousting of expectations and a negotiation of the possible. A husband and wife seldom fully meet each other's expectations, leading to "discussions" and "explosions." We have had our share of both and know that it is possible to work through them and build each other up rather than tear each other down.

Is your marriage struggling under unmet expectations you have of each other? If so, learn to compromise in love. Learn to live with each other's personality quirks and adjust your natural desires so that you better serve and please each other. Remember the direct commands of Scripture on marriage:

Husbands, love your wives.[4]

Wives, see that you respect your husbands.[5]

Learn to recognize, meet, and adjust to each other's expectations.

UNMET EXPECTATIONS FROM OUR CHILDREN

While they are growing up, our children consume the majority of our time, apart from work—and rightly so. We are called to be parents. We are called to nurture them into godly, independent adults.

However, every child becomes a master of manipulation. They plead, cajole, and demand to get their way. It's not our job as parents to give in to their every whim. In fact, when we deny our children money, clothes, cars, or privileges, we are helping them break out of their inborn selfishness and moderate their desires and expectations so they become responsible adults.

Later, when our children become adults, they still have expectations of us as their parents. Some possible expectations are:

- Financial support for education
- Freedom to move back home
- Financial support and help after a divorce
- Child care
- Emotional support
- Rescue in financial difficulties
- Taking their side in marriage difficulties

As parents, most of us will do anything within our power to help our children in all of these areas. However, when the expectations placed on us exceed reason, problems emerge.

Every child differs in how he or she views a parent's responsibility, interactions, and contributions. The two of us grew up in an era where children had almost no expectations of their parents upon adulthood. We assumed we were adults, made our choices, and lived with all the consequences.

But for the last two generations, especially in the United States, expectations have changed. Our own children have not put many expectations on us, but we know parents who struggle with their children's demands. Guilt and conflict easily develop. Your children's expectations may not be selfish, but conflict can develop under the best of circumstances.

Here are some truths to take into account when it comes to dealing with your adult children's expectations:

- All children (and grandchildren) rightly deserve your unconditional love and constant encouragement. This far outweighs any material help.
- Your children's expectations cannot control your lives.
- There will always be unmet expectations.

- Your capability to meet the expectation needs to be evaluated by both you and your children, always with compassion and consideration.
- Generosity with time and resources should govern your thinking.
- Your health and age may place natural limitations on expectations.

There will come a time when your children will need to step in to care for you, the parent. This should affect how you respond to your kids now.

UNMET EXPECTATIONS FROM SOCIETY

One of the earliest verses we committed to memory in a modern translation was Romans 12:2 from the J. B. Phillips translation: "Don't let the world around you squeeze you into its own mould, but let God re-make you so that your whole attitude of mind is changed. Thus you will prove in practice that the will of God [is] good, acceptable to him and perfect."

God condemned the people of Israel for adopting the pagan practices of the surrounding nations. He used the harshest of language to denounce their practices: prostitution, wars, false gods, immoral worship practices, and sacrificing their children. The Israelites never seemed to resist the corrupting influence of their neighbors. In fact, the story of the Old Testament can be told by reciting the corrupt practices of Israel and their eventual return to God.

We wonder at their weakness and stupidity, yet we are not so very different. We, too, slip silently into conformity with the world's ways: in money, in prestige, in lifestyle, and in thinking. This tendency is exacerbated in the lives of teens and young adults. As adults, we are blinded to our own surrender to societal thinking and ways of living.

May those who hope in you not be disgraced because of me, O Lord, the LORD Almighty; may those who seek you not be put to shame because of me, O God of Israel. — Psalm 69:6

The expectations of society must not drive us. Peter's words in his first epistle apply to us as well: "You have spent enough time in the past doing what pagans choose to do—living in debauchery, lust, drunkenness, orgies, carousing and detestable idolatry."[6] We are to be a holy people in thought and practice, so reject the pressures to conform in ways that discredit God, compromise your morality, and pollute your walk with God.

Shrug off society's expectations. Study Scripture to know what God expects of you, and live accordingly.

UNMET EXPECTATIONS FROM PEERS

The old phrase "Keeping up with the Joneses" implies a sobering truth: We are influenced by our peers in how we think, what our aspirations are, what we value, and how we live. The friendship and influence of godly friends is profoundly important in keeping us balanced and focused on God.

Scripture tells us to live in the midst of the lost but without adopting their ways. Although it is important to nurture friendships with nonbelievers so that you can influence them to faith, be wise. First Corinthians 15:33 cautions, "Do not be deceived: 'Bad company corrupts good morals'" (NASB). There are stark differences between the ideas and beliefs of believers and nonbelievers. Be sure you don't conform to actions and beliefs that would dishonor God.

These passages of Scripture, which address how to interact with nonbelievers, have been a help to us:

They think it strange that you do not plunge with them into the same flood of dissipation, and they heap abuse on you.[7]

Be wise in the way you act toward outsiders; make the most of every opportunity. Let your conversation be always full of grace, seasoned with salt, so that you may know how to answer everyone.[8]

Choose your friends well, for they will ultimately influence you with their expectations.

UNMET EXPECTATIONS FROM ONE'S PROFESSION

We all face demands in our work. Whether our jobs are in manufacturing, ministry, sales, construction, business, medicine, education, the service industry, or management, they have unique demands. Employers expect extra training, long hours, and high standards of performance and production. All compete for our time and energy.

Knowing how to respond to these demands is not easy. Our job security can depend on our availability to travel, work long hours, or change locations. To remain competitive for promotion, extra training or education may be required.

The key to responding well to these demands? Recognizing that you cannot do it all. Everyone has limitations of time, skill, and energy. For example, mothers face an unusual set of expectations. They manage households, finances, schedules, and possibly a job outside the home. Understanding and accepting that your tasks are never finished gives you great freedom.

If you feel that your profession is asking something of you that would not be good for you or your family, do what you feel that God is leading you to do, and trust the consequences to Him. At a critical point in his Air Force career, Jerry turned down a key school assignment, knowing it would reflect negatively on his record. He felt that the assignment would not be best for our family and for the spiritual influence we were having at the Air Force Academy. Strangely, the Air Force chose not to enter the decision on his record, and his career flourished.

Remember:

- No one can do it all.
- No one does everything perfectly.
- You will always live with unmet expectations.
- Ultimately, God will honor your work: "Whatever you do, do it heartily, as to the Lord and not to men."[9]

THE BOTTOM LINE

As you finish reading this chapter, you might be thinking one of the following:

Okay, now tell me something I don't know.

I still live with the expectations. You gave me no solutions.

Tell me exactly what I am supposed to do.

Sorry, we can't meet all your expectations.

Here is the bottom line: Much of the pressure you feel from unmet expectations comes from expectations you have of yourself. Thus, learning to be realistic and reasonable about your self-imposed demands is the first step. You are in control of what you do.

All other expectations are external. You do not create them. Your task is to decide which are legitimate and deserve attention and which are unrealistic and need to be ignored or deflected. Seek wisdom and discernment from God and help from others.

> *Never walk away from Wisdom — she guards your life;*
> *love her — she keeps her eye on you.*
> *Above all and before all, do this: Get Wisdom!*
> *Write this at the top of your list: Get Understanding![10]*

Trust, do good, and be wise. These priorities will never fail you.

QUESTIONS FOR REFLECTION

1. What makes having expectations from others so stressful?
2. Compare your own expectations of yourself to others' expectations of you. Which put the most pressure on you? Why are some of them unreasonable?
3. When should expectations drive you, and when should they not?
4. How can you prioritize expectations and live without guilt and self-recrimination?

CHAPTER 14

A FORWARD LOOK

My interest is in the future because I am going to spend the rest of my life there.

CHARLES FRANKLIN KETTERING

The present is never our goal; the past and the present are our means; the future alone is our goal. Thus, we are never living, but we hope to live; and looking forward always to be happy, it is inevitable that we should never be so.

BLAISE PASCAL

If you board the wrong train, it is no use running along the corridor in the opposite direction.

DIETRICH BONHOEFFER

When Jerry was dismissed from pilot training in the Air Force, we wondered what God was doing and questioned if we should stay in the Air Force. We did not have a clue as to what our next step should be. But we were young. There was still time for a new direction, and there was hope. We were believers, so we knew that theoretically God was in charge. Still, Jerry wondered if he could have worked harder or practiced more or prayed more.

In the midst of our confusion, we believed that God had a plan and we could trust Him to fulfill it. We had hope.

As people get older, the cynicism of experience and the disappointments of the past can dim their hope, making it easy to give up. Whether young or old, the way forward is through hope. Hope always relates to the future. Hope lies in what God can and will do.

If only for this life we have hope in Christ, we are to be pitied more than all men. — 1 Corinthians 15:19

ETERNAL HOPE

All hope ultimately grounds itself in the eternal hope we possess in Christ. Even the hope of healing a terminal illness is based in an eternal hope in God's love and goodness. No other hope can compare. These Scriptures describe it best:

Praise be to the God and Father of our Lord Jesus Christ! In his great mercy he has given us new birth into a living hope through the resurrection of Jesus Christ from the dead.[1]

. . . a faith and knowledge resting on the hope of eternal life, which God, who does not lie, promised before the beginning of time.[2]

God has chosen to make known among the Gentiles the glorious riches of this mystery, which is Christ in you, the hope of glory.[3]

We wait for the blessed hope—the glorious appearing of our great God and Savior, Jesus Christ.[4]

We have this hope as an anchor for the soul, firm and secure. It enters the inner sanctuary behind the curtain.[5]

Several observations from these passages ground us in the truth:

- Eternal hope is only in Christ and is evidenced by His resurrection. "If Christ has not been raised, your faith is worthless."[6]
- Eternal hope is the hope for life beyond death, for eternal life.
- The ultimate hope will be fulfilled when Christ returns.
- This hope anchors us for every event of life. It is unshakable.

When we have this eternal hope, it makes all the difference. We have observed this in several dear friends who are dying of cancer. Their doctors have told them there is no hope, yet they are experiencing incredible eternal hope. Should they fight the cancer? Should they make the best of what is ahead in their lives? Should they do everything possible to prolong their lives? They have each made somewhat different decisions.

One friend, Lorie Vincent, wrote a book on her ten-year journey with an incurable cancer. In *Fighting Disease, Not Death*,[7] she tells how she has lived double the number of years of other patients with her particular type of cancer. Often she and her husband faced the questions "Why fight it? Why not give in? Why spend the money and the effort?" Their answer? Because life is precious! As people walk with them through the "valley of the shadow of death,"[8] they see God in a different light. They experience the courage and hope that only God can give. And by experiencing that hope, they are drawn even more closely toward the God of hope.

TEMPORAL HOPE

Even when we understand, believe, and depend on this eternal hope, the question remains as to whether there *is* temporal hope and if we can expect it. We believe the answer to both questions is yes.

Temporal refers to life on earth, the here and now, as opposed to eternal life. We want hope in this life, particularly when we wrestle with questions such as:

"Is there any hope that this problem will be resolved in my lifetime?"

"Will I ever stop hurting?"

"Will things really get better?"

"How can hope be restored when it is lost?"

We can and do have temporal hope—hope for this life. It is built on God's sustaining us in the midst of our daily lives, not on events turning out as we wish.

We are writing this chapter while in a remote location with the wind blowing forcefully. We watch the trees and plants and wonder how they survive the force of the wind. They survive by two marvelous designs of God: their root systems and the flexibility of their aboveground structures. The roots spread out to give stability in all kinds of weather. The external structure bends and twists in the wind, absorbing enormous energy before it puts unbearable stress on the roots. This is a wonderful picture of what God does for us in the midst of life's storms. He provides us with secure and strong root systems. We do all we can to prepare, endure, and bend when the shock of life's storms overwhelm us. Then God does His part to give us the strength to survive. Our hope is in Him.

The following six truths give us temporal hope:

1. God promises to sustain us in every aspect of our lives.

Never will I leave you; never will I forsake you.[9]

Do not fear, for I am with you;
do not be dismayed, for I am your God.

I will strengthen you and help you;
I will uphold you with my righteous right hand.[10]

2. God answers prayer and commands us to pray over every detail of our lives. He gives miraculous answers to our prayers. We have seen God open doors, heal bodies and relationships, bring about reconciliation, and deliver people from sin, drugs, and addictions. However, God is not our servant who does everything we demand. He knows what we need and responds accordingly. Our hope rests in knowing He will meet our needs.

3. God uses every difficulty to bring about good on our behalf. Though we need to be careful not to use Romans 8:28 as a panacea for every misunderstood act of God, it is, nevertheless, a profound truth: "We know that in all things God works for the good of those who love him, who have been called according to his purpose." We have experienced many difficult times in our lives. In all of them, we have seen so much of God's goodness. We have been sustained and given hope.

4. Hope is found in a sequence of events and in the actions of God. Romans 5:3-5 shows this sequence. Suffering produces perseverance, perseverance produces character, character produces hope, and hope never disappoints. The sequence follows rejoicing in our suffering. Through suffering we are changed for the better and given hope.

5. God is sovereign over every aspect of our lives. This is a foundational truth. It is a mystery we will never fully comprehend. He knows our longings, frailties, weaknesses, and doubts. Psalm 139 reflects this as well as any passage we know:

O LORD, you have searched me
and you know me.
You know when I sit and when I rise;
you perceive my thoughts from afar.
You discern my going out and my lying down;
you are familiar with all my ways.

Before a word is on my tongue
  you know it completely, O LORD.

You hem me in — behind and before;
  you have laid your hand upon me.
Such knowledge is too wonderful for me,
  too lofty for me to attain.[11]

When Scripture says that such knowledge is "too wonderful" and "too lofty" to attain, it simply means that it is beyond human comprehension.

If I rise on the wings of the dawn,
  if I settle on the far side of the sea,
even there your hand will guide me,
  your right hand will hold me fast.[12]

My frame was not hidden from you
  when I was made in the secret place.
When I was woven together in the depths of the earth,
  your eyes saw my unformed body.
All the days ordained for me
  were written in your book
  before one of them came to be.[13]

6. God is good and seeks our ultimate good. This gives us hope every day.

Taste and see that the LORD is good; blessed is the man who takes refuge in him.[14]

A man's steps are directed by the LORD. How then can anyone understand his own way?[15]

Though an army besiege me,
my heart will not fear;
though war break out against me,
even then will I be confident.[16]

These six truths give us temporal hope—hope in this life. At times we may doubt God's goodness, but that does not change the truth. Job expressed it well: "He knows the way that I take; when he has tested me, I will come forth as gold."[17]

We can walk confidently with God in the midst of the unfinished parts of our lives. We see and believe the eternal hope while we experience the joy of His temporal hope. In this hope, we will once again find joy.

Temporal hope requires four essential ingredients:

1. Believing in the truths of God's character and eternal hope
2. Keeping going in the midst of our unfinished lives
3. Coming daily to God in surrender, petition, and praise
4. Knowing the truth of God's Word and promises

NEVER GIVE UP

Winston Churchill stands as a giant figure of the twentieth century. He was a poor student. His father sorely neglected him, though he defended his father's actions and legacy. His mother was doting, ambitious, and blatantly immoral. Churchill, who held a Deist view of God, possessed an enormous ego and lived with an inner sense of destiny, yet he failed many times in politics and endured years of depression and despair and failure. Again and again, he had reasons to quit—to give up.

In summing up his life and work, he gave his most remembered address to his alma mater, Harrow School, on October 29, 1941: "Never give in, never, never, never, never—in nothing, great and small, large or petty—never give in except to convictions of honour and good sense."[18]

Well said.

We will all face death one day, and when we die, all aspects of our lives and earthly work will be finished. But until that day, parts of our lives will remain unfinished.

We must rely on God and the power of the Holy Spirit to energize us and inspire us to never, never give up. Now is the time to determine what we can finish, what we can and must accept, and how to wait on God to finish what we cannot.

Be on your guard; stand firm in the faith; be men of courage; be strong.[19]

Stand firm. Let nothing move you. Always give yourselves fully to the work of the Lord, because you know that your labor in the Lord is not in vain.[20]

You can and must look forward. God wants you to finish well. He gives hope to overcome your past mistakes and unfinished tasks and to dream new dreams. You have real hope for now and eternity. Commit today to finishing everything God has for you to accomplish so you can walk with joy and purpose into the future.

QUESTIONS FOR REFLECTION

1. What does looking forward mean for you?
2. As you think back over the different areas we have discussed in this book, which are the ones that cry out most for your attention now?
3. What is the tension between just surviving the pressures of the moment and looking forward to what God has for you?
4. Review some of the major applications you have made from the concepts in this book. Share or record the difference this has made in your thinking or actions.

NOTES

Chapter 1: Living in the Basement
1. 2 Timothy 4:7 (MSG).

Chapter 2: Unfinished Dreams and Goals
1. Proverbs 16:9.
2. See Genesis 37.
3. This material originally appeared in Jerry White, *The Joseph Road* (Colorado Springs, CO: NavPress, 2002), 106.

Chapter 3: Unfinished Marriages
1. Colossians 3:12-14 (TLB).
2. James 3:1-2 (TLB).

Chapter 4: Unfinished Parenting
1. This illustration is taken from Jerry and Mary White, *When Your Kids Aren't Kids Anymore* (Colorado Springs, CO: NavPress, 1989), 43.
2. http://www.wmfc.org/generationaldifferenceschart.pdf.

Chapter 5: Unfinished Careers
1. Genesis 2:15.
2. Genesis 3:17-19.
3. Exodus 28:3.
4. Daniel 1:17.

Chapter 6: Unfinished Relationships
1. Robert Louis Stevenson, in *Encyclopedia of 7000 Illustrations*, WORDsearch #936.
2. Acts 15:36-40.
3. Hebrews 12:14-15.
4. Colossians 3:13.
5. Matthew 6:14-15.

Chapter 7: Unfinished Spirituality
1. John 19:30.
2. Hebrews 10:12-14 (MSG).
3. Ephesians 1:13.
4. Hebrews 5:12-14.
5. An excellent resource is *Stages of Faith: 8 Milestones That Mark Your Journey*, by Don Willett.
6. See Romans 10:9-10; 1 John 5:11-12.
7. See John 3:16; Ephesians 2:8-9.
8. Hebrews 10:25.
9. Romans 1:9-12.
10. Both of these books can be purchased at NavPress.com.
11. Galatians 5:22-23.
12. Jerry and Mary White, *When Your Kids Aren't Kids Anymore* (Colorado Springs, CO: NavPress, 1989).

Chapter 8: Unfinished Lives
1. Luke 12:15.
2. See Exodus 2–3.
3. Proverbs 17:17.
4. Psalm 139:16.
5. See 2 Samuel 12:15-23.
6. "There's a Reason," words and music by Dan Foster. Copyright by Ron Harris Music. All rights reserved.
7. Jeremiah 29:11.

Chapter 9: Unfinished Suffering
1. John 16:33 (TLB).
2. Psalm 139:13-16.
3. James 1:2-4 (NLT).
4. Isaiah 41:10.
5. See Isaiah 40:29-31.
6. Matthew 25:21.

Chapter 10: Getting a Second Wind
1. International Olympic Committee website en.bejing 2008, cn/education/stories/n2A077658.shtml, accessed February 29, 2012.

2. John Bunyan, *Pilgrim's Progress* (1678), in Charles Allen, *God's Psychiatry* (Grand Rapids, MI: Fleming-Revell, 1953), 37.
3. 2 Chronicles 21:20.
4. 1 Corinthians 9:24-27.
5. See 2 Corinthians 3:18; Romans 12:2.

Chapter 11: Defusing Time Bombs
1. Proverbs 18:19.
2. Proverbs 6:19.
3. Hebrews 12:15 (NASB).
4. Proverbs 29:22 (MSG).
5. Proverbs 19:11 (TLB).
6. James 1:19.
7. Ecclesiastes 4:4 (MSG).
8. 1 Peter 2:1 (MSG).
9. James 3:16 (NASB).
10. See Philippians 2:3.
11. Proverbs 15:18.
12. Proverbs 29:22.
13. Galatians 5:25-26.
14. Proverbs 24:28 (MSG).
15. Proverbs 16:27 (MSG).
16. See a further discussion on freezing in Jerry White, *Making Peace with Reality* (Colorado Springs, CO: NavPress, 2002), 137–152.
17. Daniel J. DeNoon, *Early Retirement, Early Death?* WebMD Health News, October 20, 2005, http://www.webmd.com/healthy-aging/news/20051020/early-retirement-early-death.
18. Romans 8:28.
19. 1 Timothy 2:7.
20. 2 Timothy 3:10.
21. Proverbs 20:5.
22. Proverbs 20:18 (MSG).

Chapter 13: The Pressure of Unmet Expectations
1. Jeremiah 31:3.
2. Colossians 2:20-21 (NLT).
3. See Ephesians 2:10.
4. Ephesians 5:25.

5. See Ephesians: 5:22,33.
6. 1 Peter 4:3.
7. 1 Peter 4:4.
8. Colossians 4:5-6.
9. Colossians 3:23 (NKJV).
10. Proverbs 4:6-7 (MSG).

Chapter 14: A Forward Look
1. 1 Peter 1:3.
2. Titus 1:2.
3. Colossians 1:27.
4. Titus 2:13.
5. Hebrews 6:19.
6. 1 Corinthians 15:17 (NASB).
7. Mark L. Vincent and Lorie L. Vincent, *Fighting Disease, Not Death* (Indianapolis: Dog Ear Publishing, 2011), see www.dogearpublishing.net.
8. Psalm 23:4.
9. Hebrews 13:5.
10. Isaiah 41:10.
11. Psalm 139:1-6.
12. Psalm 139:9-10.
13. Psalm 139:15-16.
14. Psalm 34:8.
15. Proverbs 20:24.
16. Psalm 27:3.
17. Job 23:10.
18. Winston Churchill, "Never Give In, Never, Never, Never," Wikisource, copy of actual speech, accessed October 27, 2011, en.wikisource.org/wiki/Never__GiveIn__Never__Never__Never.
19. 1 Corinthians 16:13.
20. 1 Corinthians 15:58.